The Story

of

Anuradhapura

Senani Ponnamperuma

Copyright © 2016-2020 Senani Ponnamperuma
All rights reserved.
2nd Edition
No part of this book may be reproduced or transmitted in any form or by any means, electronic or mechanical, including photocopying, recording, or by any information storage and retrieval system, without written permission from the author.

ISBN-13: 978-0-9873451-2-7
ISBN-10: 0-9873451-2-5

Cover: Bodhisattva Avalokitesvara seated in an attitude of royal ease; solid-cast gilded bronze, eyes inlaid with rock crystal. Elaborately plaited hair on top of the head inlaid with precious gems. The empty space in the center of the headdress held a miniature figure of Buddha. (8-9th century).

DEDICATION

To my children Trishan and Ashani.
Be enlightened.

CONTENTS

PART 1 - THE STORY   9
    INTRODUCTION   11
    THE ISLAND OF LANKA   13
    THE GREAT CHRONICLES   14
    THE STORY OF VIJAYA   16
    AGE OF MAJESTY   25
    AGE OF ANARCHY   67
    AGE OF REVIVAL   75
    AGE OF COLLAPSE   87
    ABANDONMENT   99
    REDISCOVERY   101

PART 2 - THE KINGDOM   103
    GOVERNMENT   105
    RELIGION   107
    ECONOMY   111
    SECURITY   113
    ARCHITECTURE   114
    SOCIETY   115
    ART   117
    SCULPTURE   119
    LITERATURE   121

PART 3 - THE SITE   125

Head from a figure of a deity, possibly female, with a high topknot, in granite. 7-8th Century.

PREFACE

I first visited the ruins at Anuradhapura as a teenager. Arriving at the railroad station on a steam train billowing clouds of black smoke, I engaged a decrepit but knowledgeable guide who owned an equally decrepit car, possibly even older than himself, and set out on a journey of exploration. This was a time before tourists when the entire site was deserted. As I clambered amongst the ruins, the only sound that disturbed the eerie stillness of the place was the chirping of a bird or two. My interest was rekindled nearly forty years later, when I took my young family on a grand tour of their ancestral homeland. Wanting it to be a cultural experience, I set about collecting information on the subject. While there was a copious amount of information about the kingdom of Anuradhapura, it was narrowly sourced, often unsubstantiated, and merely a repetition of commonly held views. Most professional works are, in general, far too technical for the average reader to comprehend.

This book relates the extraordinary story of the Anuradhapura Kingdom in an interesting and easy-to-read manner. It has taken nearly ten years to write and has been researched extensively. The book puts forward many new ideas, challenges some existing ones, and debunks others, but it never veers from the facts that have been checked and cross-checked. Not content with secondhand information, I have, in many cases, retraced facts back to their original sources. For instance, reading the original translations of the Dipavamsa, Mahavamsa, Rājāvaliya, and Pujavali, Faxian's A Record of Buddhistic Kingdoms, translations of the inscriptions of Asoka's edicts, the passage which refers to King Gajabahu in the South Indian epic Silappatikaram, the Tiruvalangadu plates by Rajendra Chola describing his father's conquest of Lanka and numerous rock inscriptions in Sri Lanka, and also many works by later authors and scholars. As usual, in any comprehensive and varied quest such as this, many new facts shed light onto little known aspects of this fascinating history and were incorporated into the developing manuscript.

Any understanding of the history of this island relies heavily on the chronicles maintained by the monks of the Buddhist monastery known as the Mahavihara. These documents, namely the Mahavamsa and Culavamsa, although noncanonical poems by nature, provide the most comprehensive insight into the history of this island. Keeping in mind that these were not intended as historical documents but rather as epic poems, their historical accuracy is, on the whole, reasonably precise. Some stories, however, while retaining a kernel of truth, have been embellished to meet the needs of the chronicler's larger narrative. This book attempts in these circumstances to expound the underlying truth. Substantive information from other sources, especially during the early periods, is almost nonexistent.

The island of Lanka during the Anuradhapura period consisted of three regions. Raja Rata was the core territory of the Anuradhapura Kingdom. Ruhunu to the south was a semiautonomous territory throughout most of the period of the Anuradhapura Kingdom, the final bastion and sanctuary for displaced rulers, and the springboard for aspiring leaders and resistance movements. Malaya was the most inaccessible, heavily forested, and mountainous interior of the island and a frequent hideout for miscreants.

While the Buddhist religion played a vital role in the development and character of this civilization, any discourse on the subject is too profound to do it justice in a book such as this and has been intentionally omitted. It is only discussed in the context of its impact on this kingdom.

The dates used in this book are those set out by Wilhelm Geiger, the German Orientalist, who translated the Mahavamsa and Culavamsa, as they adhere to the modern calendar and affix the parinibbāna of the Buddha to the generally accepted date of 483 BC. Several minor dating errors have been reconciled with information available today.

The book consists of three parts. Part 1 narrates the genesis story and then tracks the trajectory of the Anuradhapura Kingdom through the reigns of most influential rulers, stopping when necessary to elaborate on a king's impact on the development of the kingdom. Part 2 provides an overview of the administrative, religious, social, and cultural characteristics of the kingdom. Part 3 describes some of the many ruins scattered around the city of Anuradhapura.

As with my first book, The Story of Sigiriya, I researched hundreds of sources and took thousands of photographs and reviewed thousands more to find the right images for this book. I taught myself photography and desktop publishing to ensure that its presentation was vivid and vibrant. It has definitely been a very busy time, indeed. I hope you get as much joy as I have in learning of the fascinating history of the Anuradhapura Kingdom.

Senani Ponnamperuma

27th September 2017

PART 1 - THE STORY

INTRODUCTION

Sri Lanka is a teardrop-shaped island, just thirty-one kilometers off the southern coast of India. As a gateway between the East and West, it has a fascinating history dating back thousands of years. Traces of early human habitation on this little island extend nearly sixty thousand years into the distant Neolithic past. The Veddas, still found in remote parts of the island, are believed to be the descendants of these early inhabitants.

The people known today as the Sinhalese are an Indo-Aryan ethnic group who arrived from northeastern India in the fifth century BC. They are acknowledged as being the first colonizers of the island. By constructing a sophisticated and extensive system of irrigation, they transformed the arid plains of north-central Sri Lanka into a land of plenty.

The first of their great civilizations was the Anuradhapura Kingdom, which thrived for nearly one thousand four hundred years. Its capital, Anuradhapura, occupying an area of approximately forty square kilometers, was one of the largest and most resplendent cities of antiquity. Gigantic, gleaming white dagobas, such as Ruwanwelisaya, built in about 205 BC, were the largest brick structures on the face of the earth. Their size was surpassed only by the three greatest pyramids of Egypt.

The period that followed the establishment of the city in about 370 BC was soon followed by the promulgation of a common religion and the initiation of vast irrigation works, heralding the golden age of the Anuradhapura Kingdom. The country prospered, undertaking ever greater feats of engineering, art, and architecture. Her fame was world-renowned. Eager traders flocked to her ports, seeking out her treasures. Alas, miscreants, too, lusted for a share of her wealth and prosperity. They, in turn, brought wanton destruction and havoc.

During this period of nearly fourteen centuries, inspiring leaders spurred the people on to greater and grander achievements. In the interceding years, however, the country would sink into despair, racked by civil war, foreign invasions, and a string of lackluster rulers of little merit.

Photograph of India and Sri Lanka taken during the Gemini XI space mission on September 14, 1966.

THE ISLAND OF LANKA

The earliest known written reference to Sri Lanka is in the great Indian epic, the *Ramayana*. Dating to about 500 BC, it tells the tale of Rama and Sita. The *Ramayana* relates that in about 1500 BC, the demon-king Ravana kidnapped the beautiful Sita and spirited her away to the land of Lankadweepa. She was rescued by her husband, Rama, with the aid of his friend, the monkey-chief Hanuman, and a team of monkeys built a bridge from India to Sri Lanka for this purpose.

The *Dipavamsa*, written in about the fourth century as the first historical chronicle of the island, records the arrival of the first Indo-Aryans in 483 BC. Their leader, a rebel prince, named Vijaya, named the island Tâmraparnî, meaning "copper-colored palms."

The edicts of King Asoka (268–232 BC), inscribed on thirty-three stone pillars scattered throughout India, refer, in edicts 2 and 13, to medicines and missionaries being sent to Tambapanni. The Greek geographer Megasthenes, in the third century BC, called it Taprobanê. Strabo, a first-century Greek geographer, placed Taprobanê on the same parallel as the Horn of Africa and noted that it exported large quantities of ivory and tortoise shells. Pliny the Elder, who died during the eruption of Mt. Vesuvius in AD 79, recorded the visit of four Lankan envoys to Rome during the reign of Emperor Claudius Caesar (AD 41–54). Drawn disproportionately large on Claudius Ptolemy's AD 150 world map because of its importance, Tabrobana was an important trading post between East and West.

The name adopted by the Sinhalese for their country is derived from the Sanskrit word "lamka," meaning "island"—the name of the island in the ancient Indian epics the *Mahabharata* and the *Ramayana*. More importantly, the great historical chronicle of the island, the *Mahavamsa*, tells us in its genesis story that this is the name used by the deity Upulvan, sent by Buddha as the protector of Vijaya and his people. When asked by Vijaya: "What island is this, sir?" "The island of Lanka," replied Upulvan.

This painting from Udaipur, India, dating to AD 649, depicts the epic battle between Rama and Hanuman against Ravana, King of Lanka.

THE GREAT CHRONICLES

Sri Lanka is unique in that it has the world's oldest authenticated metrical chronicle of history. Spanning nearly two thousand four hundred years, it covers the reign of 182 rulers in three manuscripts: the *Dipavamsa* (Chronicle of the Island), *Mahavamsa* (Great Chronicle), and *Culavamsa* (Lesser Chronicle). The *Dipavamsa* and *Mahavamsa* cover the period from the arrival of the first Indo-Aryans in about 483 BC up to the reign of King Mahasena (AD 334–362). The *Culavamsa* continues the history until the annexation of the island by the British in 1815.

The chronology of kings, battles, and major feats of engineering described in these documents is believed to be generally accurate and can be corroborated by historical records in India and elsewhere from about 250 BC onward. Unfortunately, attempts by the authors of these documents to give credence to their stories by linking the Indo-Aryans' arrival on the island with the parinibbāna (nirvana-after-death) of the Buddha have distorted the accuracy of dates prior to this time.

These documents have proven to be invaluable to historians. If not for them, the evolution of the unique culture of this people and the builders of their most monumental structures, such as Ruwanwelisaya, Jetavanarama, Abhayagiri, and Sigiriya, would have been lost to history. No inscriptions, cornerstones, or other records of their construction exist.

The *Dipavamsa*, the oldest of the ancient chronicles, was compiled from earlier documents referred to as the *Atthakatha* commentaries—now lost to history—oral tradition, and a wealth of other records in the possession of the monks of the great Buddhist monasteries known as the viharas. It is the work of several authors, as reflected in its inconsistent style and incorrect use of language and meter. Written in Pali, the idiom of the Buddhist elite at the time, it was the first formal attempt to record a history of the island and the Buddhist religion of its people. Because it ends abruptly with the death of Mahasena, this document may have been written during his reign, at the time of the great banishment and diaspora of the monks of the Great Monastery, the Mahavihara. These monks might have been anxious to preserve their heritage in writing, which to them seemed near extinction during such a time of cataclysmic religious turmoil.

The *Dipavamsa* was initially translated by Hermann Oldenberg in 1879, nearly forty years after the much more florid *Mahavamsa*. Being a much less elegant document and having been translated many years after the *Mahavamsa*, it has never gained a wide readership.

> Listen to me! I shall relate the chronicle of the Buddha's visits to the island, the arrival of the Tooth Relic and the Bodhi tree, the advent of the Buddha's doctrine, the rise of the teachers, the spread of Buddhism in the island, and the coming of (Vijaya) the Chief of Men.
> *Dipavamsa* Preamble

The *Mahavamsa* was also written in Pali by the scholar-monk Mahanama during the reign of King Dhatusena (AD 460–478). It is an epic poem glorifying the Buddhist religion, the good deeds of kings, epic battles, invasions, court intrigues, and massive construction projects. Based on the *Dipavamsa*, it too covers the period from the arrival of the first Indo-Aryans in about 483 BC up to the reign of King Mahasena (AD 334–362). Some say that it was an intentional rearrangement and enhancement of the *Dipavamsa*.

The *Mahavamsa* was first translated into English by George Turnour in 1837. Another translation into German was done by Wilhelm Geiger in 1912, and subsequently translated back from German into English by Mabel Haynes Bode with revisions by Geiger. This version is now most commonly used.

The monk-scholars had their favorite monarchs, and of course, those whom they disliked. These biases and prejudices are sometimes reflected in their interpretation of events. The *Mahavamsa*, written immediately after twenty-seven years of subjugation by the Tamils of South India, shows a noticeable prejudice toward them. This is absent from the older *Dipavamsa*. What the *Mahavamsa* says and how it says it is just as important as what it omits. Wilhelm Geiger wrote in The Indian Historical Quarterly in 1930:

> There is a good number of fables, legends, and tales of marvels in the *Mahavamsa*, and we must in each particular case attempt to find out whether there is in the narrative a historical kernel or not. All these facts are told in the *Mahavamsa* in a sober and reliable form. We must not forget, however, that the *Mahavamsa* is not a dry chronicle in the modern sense of the word, but a poem. In a poem, embellishments and sometimes also exaggerations may occur. But within these limits I have the strong impression, and whoever reads the *Mahavamsa* without prejudice will have the same, that the author at least wished to tell the truth. He is perhaps sometimes misled by his education and by his conviction, on account of his priestly mode of viewing things, but he never tells a falsehood intentionally.

Scholars are of the opinion that the *Mahavamsa* is more authoritative than the *Dipavamsa*. However, there are significant variations in the description of events between the two documents that will be brought to the reader's attention throughout this book.

The original *Mahavamsa* was artificially delineated by Geiger at the end of Chapter 37. This was for two reasons. Firstly, the *Dipavamsa* ends at Chapter 37. Secondly, the *Mahavamsa* abruptly changes in style and timbre after Chapter 37, suggesting that this was a later work appended as a continuum to the narrative. Indeed it appears to be the work of many authors less lucid and fluent in the Pali idiom. The portion of the work beginning with Chapter 38 is now referred to as the *Culavamsa*. The *Culavamsa* was commenced in the thirteenth century and is a work of many authors. It continues the history of the island until 1815, when the island was conquered by the British. We are fortunate that these documents survived the mass destruction of monasteries over the ensuing centuries.

Two other chronicles, the *Rājāvaliya* and *Pujavali*, written in later periods, deal mostly with political events and are deemed less accurate than the *Mahavamsa* and *Culavamsa*.

THE STORY OF VIJAYA

The Vijaya legend is the foundational parable of the Sinhalese people. It provides the symbolic and historical context around which their identity is formed. It cements an intimate relationship between the people, their lineage, their religion, and the land that permeates through Sri Lankan history and culture.

The *Mahavamsa* starts the story of Vijaya with the marriage of the king of Vanga (present-day Bangladesh) to the daughter of the king of Kalinga (present-day Odisha, India). Their daughter, Suppadevi, is described as "very fair and amorous," and it was prophesied that she was to consummate a "union with a lion."

A 21st century painting portraying a dramatized rendition of Vijaya's landing.

Being a free-spirited woman, she disguised herself, escaped the palace, and joined a caravan headed for Magadha. While she was traveling through a forest in Lala, in what is today central Bangladesh, a lion pounced on the caravan. The lion, upon seeing Suppadevi, was smitten; remembering the prophecy, she did not resist its affection and was carried off to its lair. From this union, she gave birth to a son and a daughter. She named her son Sinhabahu, meaning "lion armed," because it was said that he had limbs like a lion. She named her daughter Sihasivali.

At age sixteen, the young man questioned his mother, saying, "wherefore are you and our father so different, dear mother?" She told him everything. When he asked, "why do we not go forth from here?" She answered, "thy father has closed the cave up with a rock."

Sinhabahu, his mother, and his sister finally escaped the lair. Covering their nakedness with branches and leaves, they traveled a great distance until they came upon a village whose inhabitants offered them food and refuge. They were eventually taken to the local king, who discovered Suppadevi's true identity and, being childless, adopted her and her children. Meanwhile, the lion, deeply grieved by the loss of his family, scoured the countryside for them, ravaging village after village in search of his family.

Finally, in desperation, the villagers petitioned the king: "a lion ravages thy country; ward off this danger, O king!" But no one in his kingdom was brave enough to face the fearsome lion. The king offered a large bounty: first one thousand, then two thousand, and finally three thousand coins to any person who rid his kingdom of the lion. The reward announcement was paraded through the streets on the back of an elephant, the proclamation reading, "let him who brings the lion receive these!"

Locations of the Vanga, Kalinga, Pundra, and Pandya kingdoms and Lanka; the red dot identifies where Vijaya is believed to have first landed in Lanka.

Twice did Sinhabahu's mother restrain him, but on the third occasion, unknown to her, he accepted the bounty. The king, upon hearing that his adopted son, Sinhabahu, was up to the challenge, proclaimed: "if thou shalt take the lion, I will give thee at once my kingdom."

Sinhabahu tracked the lion back to his lair. The lion, upon seeing his son, was overcome with great affection and came forward to greet him. The son shot an arrow at his father—not once, not twice, but three times—but each arrow rebounded off his father's forehead, deflected by a father's deep love for his son. But when the old lion grew weary and became wrathful, an arrow finally pierced him, killing him. Sinhabahu produced the head and mane of the slain lion as proof that the deed had indeed been done. At about the same time, news reached Sinhabahu that his grandfather, the king of Vanga, had passed away. Handing his newly won kingdom to his stepfather, a local prince whom his mother had married, Sinhabahu returned with his sister to Vanga. Ascending the throne there, he founded a new city, Sinhapura, and married his sister, who bore him twins: Vijaya, the firstborn, and a younger brother, Sumitta.

The *Mahavamsa* then picks up the story of Vijaya as a young man. It records that Prince Vijaya and a band of his followers indulged in "evil conduct and intolerable deeds of violence," disrupting the peace and tranquility of the kingdom. Sinhabahu's subjects demanded that his wayward son be executed. The aging Sinhabahu, who loved his errant son dearly, could not bring himself to do this. Sadly, the old king rounded up Vijaya and seven hundred of his followers, had their heads half-shaven as a sign of humiliation and loss of freedom, placed them aboard ships, and banished them from his kingdom.

During the voyage, the ships carrying the wives and children of Vijaya's party were lost in a storm and were never seen again. After sailing for some time, Vijaya and his men finally reached a large island that he promptly named "Tâmraparnî" (copper-colored palms) after the color of the soil that stained the palms of their hands and the soles of their feet. Vijaya's first encounter upon landing is said to have been with the deity Upulvan, sent by a dying Buddha to provide protection to Vijaya and his followers. Vijaya is believed to have landed around 483 BC.

His second encounter was far less sanguine. He met Kuveni, queen of the Yakkhas, a dark-skinned people of *Ramayana* legend and the original indigenous inhabitants of the island. Using her magical powers, she transformed herself into a lovely sixteen-year-old maiden and seduced Vijaya. Falling in love with Vijaya, she betrayed her people and helped him slaughter them, saying to him, "all the Yakkhas must be slain, or else the Yakkhas will slay me, for it was through me that your men have taken up their dwelling in Lanka." Kuveni bore him a son and a daughter, and he and Kuveni reigned over the land for many years. His ministers, however, were eager that Vijaya be consecrated king and convinced him to discard Kuveni and seek instead "a maiden of a noble house" from India to be his queen, thus legitimizing his hold on his new kingdom. Kuveni, heartbroken, took her two children and fled into the jungle, where she came upon remnants of her old peoples, who promptly murdered her. (In an alternate narrative, Kuveni throws herself off a large rock known as Yakdessa Gala, imploring the gods to curse Vijaya for his cruelty and to prevent any of his children from ever ruling the country.) Her uncle, taking pity on her children, helped them escape into the hinterland, where they are said to have become the ancestors of the Veddas.

Vijaya married a Pandyan princess from Madurai in South India. The Pandyan king also decreed that maidens be provided for all of Vijaya's ministers and that their families be duly compensated for the loss of their daughters. Ninety-nine royal princesses, eighteen clans, and one thousand other persons were sent by the Pandyan king. Age and marriage seem to have mellowed Vijaya, for he is said to have reigned in "peace and righteousness" for thirty-eight years.

Vijaya died without an heir, thus fulfilling the curse of Kuveni. Sumitta, his brother and chosen successor, was summoned from Sinhapura, but by then he was an old and feeble man. Thus Sumitta's son, Panduvasudeva, arrived instead with a retinue of thirty-two youths of noble blood. He was followed by his new queen consort, a princess from Pundra (a kingdom around what is now West Bengal, Bangladesh, and Bihar), as well as thirty-two female attendants for the nobles to wed. These noble migrants formed the basis for a ruling elite class and cemented the northeastern Indian bias of the local population and the Indo-Aryan domination of the island of Lanka.

The Vijaya story, part fable and part fact, sets out from the very outset to clearly differentiate the Sinhalese, with their Buddhist culture, from their Dravidian neighbors in southern India as well as from the local indigenous people. This is strengthened by the kingships being passed not

Votive figurine (mother goddess) in terracotta date unknown probably pre-Vijayan (i.e. before 5th Century BC)

to a descendent from Vijaya's union with Kuveni or with the Pandyan princess but back to a direct descendent of Sinhabahu.

Examining the Vijaya narrative reveals some interesting insights.

Suppadevi having sired children from a union with a lion, probably means that she was kidnapped by a bandit leader named "Sinha" (lion), who took her as his prize and made her his wife. The *Dipavamsa* merely states that she cohabited with a lion dwelling in the wilderness. The *Mahavamsa* embellished the story somewhat.

Vijaya's encounter with Upulvan on a mission from Buddha is no doubt a poetic license to link the story with Buddhism from the very outset. This attempt by the ancient writers to link Vijaya's arrival on the island with a momentous religious event—namely, the date on which the Buddha passed away and attained parinibbāna in 483 BC—is a historical fabrication that has distorted the true time of Vijaya's arrival in Lanka. It did, however, give the chroniclers a convenient base date from which to commence their history of the island. Using this chronological measure of time, the ancient authors fixed the time of Vijaya's arrival on the island as 483 BC. Although we have no way of validating this, it is reasonable to assume that Vijaya probably arrived within fifty years of that date.

There are various interpretations of the locations of the sites referred to in this story. Some place Vijaya's origin in northeastern India, near modern-day Odisha and Bangladesh, while others suggest northwestern India, near present-day Gujarat. All seem to agree, however, that Indo-Aryan settlers from northern India sailed to Sri Lanka. The generally held view is that they were from northeastern India (the people of Vanga were known for their seafaring skills). The proximity of the various kingdoms mentioned in the story lends added credence to this argument. Recent genetic affinities studies indicate that there is a very high percentage of Bengali contribution (i.e., northeastern India, near present-day Odisha and Bangladesh) to the Sinhalese gene pool. There is no such contribution from northwest India.

Vijaya and his companions arrived in Sri Lanka without female companions, the boats carrying the wives and children having been lost at sea. It is reasonable to assume, therefore, that they consorted with local women and that they had progeny. Vijaya went on to marry a Pandyan princess from Madurai in southern India. Interestingly, there is some evidence to suggest that the Pandya ruling class at the time might have been of Aryan stock, most probably from northwestern India, who had established themselves in the predominantly Tamil territories of South India. Vijaya's ministers and the Pandyan king might have known of this common affinity and thus agreed to this union. Furthermore, the infusion of such a large Pandyan émigré population was a godsend for the little community establishing itself on the island. The Pandyans were experts at riverbank agriculture and water management. These skills and other talents they brought with them were put to good use by Vijaya's heirs.

The *Dipavamsa*, the oldest of the chronicles, makes no mention of Kuveni. This might be a later embellishment to the story to delineate the northern Indian migrants from the local indigenous population. There are many parallels between the Vijaya story and some of the earliest Buddhist literature known as the Jataka stories—namely, the *Padakusalamanava Jataka*, *Valahassa Jataka*, and *Devaldhamma Jataka*. The similarity between the Vijaya and Kuveni story and that of Ulysses and Circe in Homer's *Odyssey* may point to its origin in proto–Indo-European mythology.

The description of the dark-skinned native inhabitants as Yakkhas (devils and demons), alien to the lighter-skinned northern Indians, provided justification for their annihilation. The later addition of Vijaya's relationship with Kuveni might be an attempt to explain the remnant indigenous population whose members still inhabit remote parts of the island to the present day.

This foundation myth sets out to clearly delineate the Sinhalese with their Buddhist culture from their Dravidian neighbors in South India, as well as from the local indigenous people. This intimate relationship between the people, their religion, and the land permeates Sri Lankan history and culture.

Interestingly, the Sinhalese, the lion race, tie their identity to Sinhabahu and not to his son Vijaya, who, common sense suggests, would have been the natural totemistic founder of the Sinhalese people.

It is by the name "Simhala," or its dialectical forms such as "Sinhala," that the island and its people are generally referred to in classical Sanskrit, Pali, and Sinhalese literature, and it is by this name that the majority of its inhabitants identify themselves today. Interestingly, lions have not inhabited the island since prehistoric times. They were, however, present in northeastern India in Kalinga and Vanga, giving further credence to the story of the origins of these people.

The story of Vijaya, whether a pure fabrication or based on fact, is the framework of the Sinhalese ethos, culture, language, religion, and identity.

Vijaya and Kuveni depicted in the Ajanta Caves, India circa 5th century AD.

5–6th century carving believed to be that of a royal family

AGE OF MAJESTY

The Anuradhapura Kingdom was founded in 370 BC by King Pandukabhaya, the great-grandnephew of Vijaya. Located in Raja Rata, the semiarid north-central region of Sri Lanka, this kingdom was the most powerful of three principalities and, from time to time, exerted its hegemony over the lesser princedoms of Ruhunu and Malaya, farther to the south. An ample and reliable water supply was the lifeblood of this hydraulic civilization. As a result, the construction and maintenance of irrigation works was an obsessive preoccupation of these people. Almost every depression on the surface of the land was dammed and converted into a water reservoir. These were interconnected with an extensive system of canals and channels to distribute the precious liquid throughout the kingdom. As a consequence of their enterprise, large tracts of previously infertile land were progressively irrigated and brought under cultivation. The ensuing surpluses in agriculture and the subsequent prosperity supported a large community of officials, monks, artisans, traders, and scholars.

So enamored were these people and their kings with their new Buddhist religion that they collectively abhorred bearing arms and did not maintain a regular army, preferring instead to invest their energies in vast irrigation projects and monasteries—viharas—glorifying their religion. These viharas, with vast tracts of prime land, increasingly dominated production and economic activity, enhancing their wealth and influence substantially. The Chinese chronicler Faxian, in AD 411, enthusiastically described these huge establishments housing more than fifteen thousand monks and their mighty dagobas, some almost as big as the pyramids that soared majestically into the sky. He also noted that the streets were well maintained, with four principal avenues dividing the city. He added that wealthy Indian, Mediterranean, and Persian merchants and Sinhalese nobles lived in richly adorned multistoried houses, and that the city had lamp-lit streets; numerous ponds, baths, and parks; piped water, and an efficient sewerage system using recycled water.

This golden age of the Anuradhapura Kingdom spanned nearly nine hundred years, during which; a multiethnic society led by many visionary and inspirational leaders spurred the people to great feats of engineering, architecture, literature, and arts unrivaled by any other Asian civilization except those of India and China. In time, however, they would pay dearly for their reluctance to bear arms and the neglect of their army.

Pandukabhaya (377–307 BC)
Founder of Anuradhapura

Early settlement of the island was restricted to small villages and towns in the arid northern part of the island. However, erratic monsoonal rains, a burgeoning population, and the introduction of rice cultivation necessitated the need to secure a reliable water supply. The original capital Tampabanni and a subsequent one named Upa-tissa-Nuwera were soon found unsuitable. In 437 BC, on the advice of a soothsayer, King Pandukabhaya moved his capital to a settlement located on a fertile plain deep in the interior. This settlement had been founded by a kinsman of Vijaya's named Anuradha, and his town was called "Anuradhagama": Anuradha's village. The village headman at the time, the granduncle of the king, was also named Anuradha. Furthermore, because this settlement had been founded under the constellation Anuradha, the new city was aptly named Anuradhapura, "pura" meaning "city."

Pandukabhaya's city was a model of urban planning, with precincts set aside for various groups such as huntsmen, scavengers, and heretics as well as foreigners. It featured hostels, hospitals, a Jain monastery named Tittharama (which would play a defining role in the reign of Vattagamani-abhaya in 43 BC), and cemeteries for the higher and lower castes. Pandukabhaya appointed able administrators to run his kingdom and set up a village community-based system of government that survives to this day. To ensure a reliable food and water supply for his kingdom, he undertook the first large-scale irrigation and agricultural projects on the island. By building massive reservoirs, he transformed the hostile land into one of plenty. By the end of Pandukabhaya's reign, Anuradhapura was a burgeoning city, and the Sinhalese were the entrenched power of the island.

> He laid out also four suburbs as well as the Abhaya tank, the common cemetery, the place of execution, and the chapel of the Queens of the West, the banyan tree of Vessavana, and the Palmyra palm of the Demon of Maladies, the ground set apart for the Yonas [Greeks] and the house of the Great Sacrifice; all these he laid out near the west gate.
> (*Mahavamsa* Chap. X, verse 89–90)

Pandukabhaya's reign is fixed at seventy years, giving him a lifespan of 107 years. This and the subsequent sixty-year reign of his son Mutasiva (307–247 BC) are unrealistic. It appears that the authors of the ancient chronicles stretched the reigns of these rulers to force synchronicity between the arrival of Vijaya and the parinibbāna of the Buddha—thus providing an auspicious beginning to the nation.

Devanampiya-tissa (247–207 BC)
Introduction of Buddhism

Tissa, later known by the honorific Devanampiya-tissa, was the grandson of Pandukabhaya. At the time of Tissa's ascension to the throne, Emperor Asoka (268–232 BC) ruled as the supreme overlord of most of the Indian subcontinent. Asoka's bloody conquest of Kalinga in 261 BC had been an epiphany for him. Having witnessed the carnage he himself had wrought, which left more than one hundred thousand dead, Asoka forsook violence and embraced the teachings of the Buddha.

For many years, Tissa had keenly cultivated the friendship of Asoka, exchanging numerous gifts with him. In one such instance, the *Mahavamsa* tells us, Asoka responded to Tissa's lavish gifts of pearls, sapphires, rubies, and other precious gems by exclaiming, "here I have no such precious things." A commentary to the *Mahavamsa*, quoting other ancient sources, informs us that Asoka enquired from Tissa's envoys about the abhiseka, or royal consecration rites of monarchs in their homeland. When informed that there were no such rites, Asoka resolved to send his friend all the trappings necessary for such a ceremony. Asoka's gifts included, among other things, a fan, a crown, ear ornaments, necklaces, a parasol, shoes, a turban, and, most interesting, a royal virgin. Asoka also sent a personal message entreating Tissa to join his new religion. Tissa conveniently ignored this plea. With Asoka's acquiescence, about a year after Tissa's original ascendance to leadership, he was reconsecrated using the lavish fitments of kingship provide by Asoka. The *abhiseka* ceremony and the parasol, or *senachatra*, were in time to become important symbols of kingship. Tissa also adopted the name bestowed on him by Asoka: Devanampiya-tissa (Tissa, friend of the gods).

The *Mahavamsa* tells us that in the second year of Tissa's rule, while the king was hunting alone in the mountains of Cetiyagiri (known today as "Mihintale," or Mahinda's Mountain), he came upon a hermit who addressed him thusly: "come hither, Tissa." The king was taken aback by this flagrant disregard for his regal presence. The hermit then declared, "recluses we are, O great King, disciples of the King of Dharma." Remembering Asoka's letter, Tissa realized that this might be a messenger from Asoka and engaged in several lengthy discourses, one of which is recorded in the *Mahavamsa* (Chapter 14) thusly:

"What name does this tree bear, O king?"

"This tree is called a Mango."

"Is there yet another Mango besides this?"

"There are many mango trees."

"And are there yet other trees besides this mango and the other mangos?"

"There are many trees, sir; but those are trees that are not mangoes."

"And are there, besides the other mangoes and those trees which are not mangoes, yet other trees?"

"There is this mango tree, sir."

"Thou hast a shrewd wit, O ruler of men!

"Hast thou kinsfolk, O king?"

"There are many, sir."

"And are there also some, O king, who are not kinsfolk of thine?"

"There are yet more of those than of my kin."

"Is there yet any one besides the kinsfolk and the others?"

"There is yet myself, sir."

"Good! Thou hast a shrewd wit, O ruler of men!"

Satisfied with the king's quick wit and intelligence, the thera Mahinda preached to Tissa.

The first sermon was preached to a congregation consisting mainly of the ladies of the royal household (the harem) in a specially built pavilion in the royal palace compound. The common people, too, clamored to hear the missionaries preach. Because the palace grounds were too small, an elephant stable was readied for this purpose. The crowds grew even larger that the next congregation gathered on the grounds of Nandana Park outside the capital. (This park was to play a pivotal role in Sri Lankan history nearly a millennium later.) That evening, Mahinda wished to return to the quiet solitude of Mihintale, but the king convinced him to use the royal Mahameghavana Park, to the south of the city,

This rock crystal reliquary, dated to around 307-267 BC, is believed to have been found in the Thuparama dagoba. It has a cylindrical cavity bored into the top within which a relic would have been stored, safely held within by a now-absent stopper that was carved as a six-tiered umbrella. Given its age and the claimed location of its discovery, this reliquary may be an accurate representation of the original Thuparama built by Devanampiya-tissa.

as a refuge instead. The following morning, the king gifted this park to Mahinda. Here was laid the foundation of the Mahavihara, the greatest Buddhist monastic establishment in the world. It is said that the king and forty thousand of his subjects converted to the new religion.

On hearing of Tissa's conversion, Asoka also presented Tissa with relics from the Buddha. These included the right collarbone of the Buddha, which was enshrined in the Thuparama, the first dagoba to be built on the island, and the Alms Bowl of the Buddha, which became a vital talisman of the right to kingship and was kept in the royal palace. He also dispatched Samghhamitta, Mahinda's sister, who had become a nun, with a sapling of the sacred Bodhi tree under which Buddha had attained enlightenment. The arrival of Samghhamitta and the sapling were received with great fanfare, and the plant was installed on a high terrace in Mahameghavana Park, where it still stands today.

With keen royal patronage, Buddhism quickly eclipsed Brahmanism, Jainism, and all other religions to become the preeminent religion of the Sinhalese nation. By its wider acceptance, Buddhism became the thread that bound the people together with a common religion, language, and script, hastening the political and cultural unification of the country. The adoption of Buddhism further delineated the Sinhalese from their South Indian neighbors

A 20th century depiction of the arrival of the Bodhi Tree.

Contrary to the impression conveyed by the *Mahavamsa*, however, the new religion was not universally adopted. The new religion had little effect on one person in particular: Tissa's queen, intent on ensuring her son's succession to the throne, plotted to assassinate Mahanaga, Tissa's brother, who was next in line of succession. She sent him a gift of delicious mangoes, of which the topmost fruit she had poisoned. As fate would have it, Mahanaga was supervising the construction of a reservoir, and the young prince was by his side on the construction site. Mahanaga, unaware that the mango was poisoned, gave the topmost fruit to his nephew, who ate it and died instantly. Mahanaga, fearing for his life, fled for the sanctuary of Ruhunu and set himself up as ruler there.

Devanampiya-tissa is a pivotal character in Sri Lankan history. It was during his reign that Buddhism was introduced to the island and molded the distinct culture that developed on this island.

Sena and Guttika (177–155 BC)
First "Foreign" Rulers

> Two Damilas, Sena and Guttika, sons of a freighter who brought horses hither, conquered the king Sūratissa, at the head of a great army and reigned both together twenty-two years justly.
> *Mahavamsa* (Chapter. XXI, verse 10)

It is here that we first see the use of the term "Damila", which deserves some clarification. The concept of ethnicity, so pervasive in the modern world, was not manifest in those early days. Diversity in the eyes of the authors of the ancient chronicles was, initially, more one of being non-Buddhist than of race or color. Therefore, when the term "Damila" was used in these texts, it usually meant "foreign," that is "not one of us," and by default, this included the South Indian Dravidian ethnic group referred to today as Tamils. These people, by nature of their religion and geography, were alien to the Buddhist authors of the chronicles. It was only later that this word evolved into a more specific pejorative for people of South India known as the Tamils. We do not see this word used in the genesis story of Vijaya, neither during his travels through South India nor in his marriage to a princess from the same region. It first appears after Buddhism was introduced to the island and then mainly when rulers appeared to be secular in their outlook and not partial to the Buddhist religion of the Mahavihara.

Keeping this in mind, the *Dipavamsa* tell us that Sena and Guttika were two Damila princes while the *Mahavamsa* tells us that they were two Damilas, the sons of a horse trader. Interestingly, the name Guttika means guardian or watchman in Pali, and the word "Sena" means army and is the root for words such as *senapati*, a minister of war. These positions were usually held by relatives of the sovereign. In this light, we could interpret the account in the *Dipavamsa* to read that they were two non-Buddhist princes who usurped power and ruled justly. In the *Mahavamsa* account, we are told that Sena and Guttika were a horse trader's sons. While they may well have been Tamil, it has also led to speculation that they might even have been Persian, for most horses were imported from Persia. Neither the *Dipavamsa* nor *Mahavamsa* suggests an overseas invasion of any sort.

It is more likely that in about 177 BC, two "foreigners," one of whom might have been the king's chief of the army and the other his palace bodyguard, deposed **Sura-tissa (187–177 BC)**, the younger brother of Devanampiya-tissa. They were secular rulers who governed justly for twenty-two years and were ousted by **Asela (155–145 BC)**, a nephew of Devanampiya-tissa.

Pure silk panel based on a mural at Avadiyar Temple near Villuputam, India depicting the story of the cow and the bell.

Elara (145–101 BC)
An Interloper Renowned for His Virtuousness

Elara is an enigmatic figure in Sri Lankan history. The *Dipavamsa* and *Mahavamsa* both concur that he was a prince of noble birth who seized the throne from the reigning monarch, Asela. They also state that he governed with exemplary virtuousness for forty-four years and was ousted by a prince named Dutugamunu. From this point onward, their accounts diverge significantly. The *Dipavamsa* narrates (ch. XVIII, v 49):

> A Prince, Elara by name, having killed Asela, reigned righteously for forty-four years.

The *Mahavamsa*, on the other hand, embellishes its story with many nuances. The equivalent passage in the *Mahavamsa* (ch. XXI, v 13–14) reads:

> A Damila of noble descent, named Elara, who came hither from the Chola country to seize on the kingdom, ruled when he had overpowered king Asela, forty-four years, with even justice towards friend and foe, on occasions of disputes at law.

A key distinction in the *Mahavamsa* story is its assertion that Elara was a Damila who came from the Chola country. The *Dipavamsa* makes no such allegation. Although the word "Damila" was usually used to denote a foreigner, in this particular instance, the *Mahavamsa* intentionally uses the phrase "Damila from Chola country" as a veiled pejorative to assert that he was a Tamil usurper from South India. Having made this assertion, the author immediately sets about restituting Elara's image with effusive tales of his virtuousness:

> At the head of his bed was a bell attached to a rope so that anyone who desired a judgement of law might ring it. The King had one son and a daughter. His son, while on the way to Tissa Wewa, unintentionally killed a young calf lying by the roadway by driving the wheel of his chariot over its neck. The cow came and rang the bell, and the king caused his son's head to be severed from his body with that same wheel. (*Mahavamsa* ch. XXI, v 15–18)

This account of Elara's wisdom in the *Mahavamsa* is identical to the story of King Manuneethi Cholan and the Cow and the Bell, written in the second-century South Indian epic *Silappatikaram* nearly three hundred years before the *Mahavamsa*. Interestingly, the Sri Lankan king Gajabahu

(AD 174–196) is also mentioned in this epic. It is possible that the author of the *Mahavamsa* used the Manuneethi Cholan story to illustrate the virtues of a just ruler. This and other stories of Elara's righteousness might have been intended as recompense for stretching the truth about his "foreign" lineage.

Elara reigned less than a century after Buddhism had been introduced to the island. There was still a large contingent of people, royalty and commoners alike, who adhered to other religions, such as Brahmanism and Jainism. It is most likely that Elara was a non-Buddhist member of the royal lineage who usurped power from a ruler named Asela. Elara governed justly, as a secular ruler, respecting the religions of all his subjects, and offered no special favors or royal patronage to the Buddhist clergy. Loath to be untruthful, both ancient chronicles acknowledge his virtuousness.

The *Mahavamsa* was written nearly six hundred years after Elara's rule. During this time, a firm view had taken root that only a Buddhist king, and particularly only one descended from an authenticated royal bloodline, had the legitimate right to rule the kingdom. Because Elara did not meet these criteria—and for ideological expediency—he was branded an archenemy of the Sinhala Buddhist nation by medieval writers intent on inflaming Sinhala nationalism. (The seventeenth-century Sinhala chronicle the *Rājāvaliya* goes so far as to describe him as an impious monster and a defiler of temples.)

There is no corroborating evidence, whatsoever, to support the assertion made by some that Elara was the mythical Manuneethi Cholan.

Dutugamunu (101–77 BC)
Nation Builder and Hero of the Mahavamsa

Gamini Abhaya, more commonly known by his honorific Dutugamunu, was the great-grandson of Mahanaga, Devanampiya-tissa's younger brother, who had fled Anuradhapura after the queen had tried to poison him nearly a hundred years earlier.

He was the eldest son of Kakavanna-tissa, the wise and wily ruler of Ruhunu, a princedom in the far south of the island. Kakavanna-tissa retained the independence of Ruhunu by shrewdly maintaining a strong military stance against Elara while at the same time fostering a tacit truce between himself and Elara, acknowledging the latter as overlord of Lanka.

From an early age, Prince Gamini displayed an outright hostility and loathing for Elara. Skilled in the art of handling elephants and horses and an expert swordsman and archer, he surrounded himself with a band of like-minded nationalists, and on three occasions, demanded permission, from his father the king, to wage war against Elara. The old king vehemently refused him each time. Chafing under his father's restraints, Gamini, in a fit of pique, muttered "if my father were a man, he would not speak like a woman" and sent him a set of female garments. King Kakavanna-tissa was outraged and immediately ordered that his insolent son be tethered in chains. Gamini absconded and went into hiding in the mountains of Malaya country. The impetuous young prince thus earned the peoples' sobriquet "Duttha Gamini" (bad or disobedient Gamini), later simplified as Dutugamunu.

On the death of Kakavanna-tissa, leadership did not readily pass to his eldest son, Dutugamunu. His younger brother Saddha-tissa challenged him. The *Mahavamsa* describes vividly the epic battles between them. In the final battle, Dutugamunu was victorious, and Saddha-tissa fled the battlefield with Dutugamunu in hot pursuit. Saddha-tissa sought refuge in a vihara and hid under the bed of the head monk who spread a cloak over the bed to hide him. Dutugamunu followed and asked, "where is Tissa?" The monk not wishing to lie, replied: "he is not in the bed, great king." Dutugamunu knew that his brother was hiding under the bed but dared not violate the sanctuary of the vihara. So he placed guards around the premises and withdrew. The monks then placed Saddha-tissa on top of the bed, covered him with a garment, and carried him out as though they were carrying a dead monk to a funeral pyre. But Dutugamunu was not fooled and said loudly, "Tissa, you are safe there on the bed of our family deities. It is not for me to take you by force from them. But you should forever emulate the virtues of our family deities." The significance of this utterance will be revisited later.

Saddha-tissa escaped, but later through the intervention of the Sangha, the two brothers were reconciled, and Saddha-tissa served his elder brother loyally thereafter. Elara, in the meantime, had not been idle. His forces had steadily encroached along the northern perimeter of the principality.

There was no time to waste. Dutugamunu was determined to wage war on Elara. His war would be a holy war—a war for the glorification of his religion. To drive home this point, he publicly installed a relic of the Buddha in his spear as a holy talisman for the battle ahead. To give further credence to his cause, he assembled five hundred monks who were to accompany him on the journey north. Motivated by a cause greater than their own, the troops rallied around him ready to rid the country of the impostor, Elara, and restore their religion to its former preeminence.

Mounted on his mighty war elephant, Kandula, and flanked by of his most trusted warriors, Dutugamunu set out to war. His first task was to dislodge nine of Elara's garrisons that had encroached on Ruhunu territory. This he did with relative ease. But as he progressed northward, resistance grew more unyielding. All but one of his next fourteen encounters were not with Elara forces. Instead, they were with local chieftains who opposed him. Most notable amongst these was his own half-brother, Dighajantu, who had defected to Elara. Suffice it to say that even by the *Mahavamsa*'s own account, there was no popular uprising against Elara. Dutugamunu's progress was challenged all the way to the gates of the capital.

The first crucial battle took place at Vijitanagara, near present-day Polonnaruwa. The garrison there defended itself tenaciously. Repeated attempts by Dutugamunu's forces to breach its defenses were thwarted. Even Kundula, Dutugamunu's mighty war elephant, while attempting to batter down the gates of the fortress came to grief when molten pitch was hurled down onto him from the walls above. Bellowing in agony, the mightly elephant fled and doused his burns in a pool of water.

It took Dutugamunu's forces four months to capture the fort. In the final battle, Kundula the war-elephant, successfully battered down the fortress gates and the attackers entered the fort, and wrought carnage on the survivors.

Until this point, Elara's main army at Anuradhapura had not confronted Dutugamunu. Elara was holding them in reserve, intent on letting the armies of his proxies wear down Dutugamunu forces on their exhausting march toward the capital. Attrition among Dutugamunu's troops might have been high, because he chose not to push home his advantage but elected instead to camp twenty-nine kilometers away from the capital and replenish his army for the battle ahead. Elara, in turn, was reluctant to take the offensive because after the fall of Vijitanagara, his key general, Dighajantu, had suggested that they bolster their forces with reinforcements before doing further battle with Dutugamunu. These troops had yet to arrive. Several months passed before Elara, finally weary of an opponent growing stronger so close to his capital, consulted his ministers who advised him to take the fight to Dutugamunu. The *Rājāvaliya* narrates eloquently:

> Elara sent a letter written in the following terms: "King Dutugamunu, what profiteth it you to stay at Kasagulugama? Come out to-morrow to battle". When the letter sent by Elara was brought to Dutugamunu, he read it, and in reply he wrote, "we were coming; - come ye."

As in the game of chess, which originated in ancient India, the rulers of war were governed by the Kshatriya code of chivalry in which the objective of a battle was to capture or slay the opponent's commander. The defenders' role was to prevent this. In this way, unnecessary bloodshed was avoided. Well aware of this, Dutugamunu followed the advice of his mother and devised an elaborate ruse. The Sinhalese set up thirty-two effigies of Dutugamunu, complete with the royal parasol, in various places along the battlefront. As expected, Dighajantu, Elara's battlefield commander, attacked what he thought to be Dutugamunu, the commander of the Sinhalese army. It was a ruse. He attacked the second, but that, too, was a trick. After several failed attempts in which his army was slowly depleted, Dighajantu finally found Dutugamunu. Dutugamunu's adjutant parried with Dighajantu and slew him. Upon hearing of the death of their elite commander, Elara's army broke and fled toward the capital. Dutugamunu's army gave chase and caused mayhem among their foes. Elara, too, who had taken to the field but had not confronted Dutugamunu—not being seen as equal in rank to a king—fled the scene. Dutugamunu let it be known to his troops that he alone would confront Elara, observing the Kshatriya's code of chivalry. It was to be a battle between equals. The *Mahavamsa* relates the story:

> Near the south gate of the city the two kings fought; Elara hurled his dart, Gamini evaded it; he made his own elephant pierce Elara's elephant with his tusks and hurled his dart at Elara; and he fell there, with his elephant. When he had thus been victorious in battle and had united Lanka under one parasol he marched, with chariots, troops and beasts for riders, into the capital. In the city he caused the drum to be beaten, and when he had summoned the people he celebrated the funeral rites for king Elara. On the spot where his body had fallen he burned it with the catafalque, and there did he build a monument and ordain worship. And even to this day the princes of Lanka, when they draw near to this place, silence their music because of this worship.

Bhalluka, Dighajantu's nephew, whom Elara had summoned, arrived with a relieving army just seven days after Elara's death and was soon routed near a small village called Kolambahalaka. Dutugamunu was now the undisputed overlord of all of Lanka.

Like Asoka, after the carnage at Kalinga, Dutugamunu too felt deep remorse for the loss of human life he had caused. After all, he had waged his campaign for the glorification of the religion of the Buddha, who had proclaimed that all manner of killing was sinful. Dutugamunu was consoled by the argument that although he had taken life, the effort of his good deeds so far and into the future would intercede and negate the worst of his transgressions. There would be hope for him still in the afterlife. Mollified, Dutugamunu went on to rule as a Dharmaraja - a just king - devoting the rest of his life to advancing the cause of Buddhism and the well-being of his people. His religious zeal and devotion might even have surpassed those of his forefather Devanampiya-tissa. He built the largest dagoba to date, the Mirisawetiya, and then went on to better himself by building the magnificent nine-storied Lovamahapaya, the Brazen Palace, for the clergy. In his final act of piety, he commenced construction of the massive Ruwanwelisaya dagoba. No doubt, he was a favorite of the *Mahavamsa*.

Of the thirty-seven chapters of the *Mahavamsa*, eleven cover Dutugamunu's life. No other ruler, not even Devanampiya-tissa, warranted this much attention from the *Mahavamsa*. Its treatment of this king is thus worthy of further analysis.

Dutugamunu's nemesis was Elara. The *Dipavamsa* and *Mahavamsa* concur that Elara was a just ruler of noble birth, but they diverge on his ethnicity. There is no compelling evidence to suggest that Elara, as stated by the *Mahavamsa*, was a Tamil (Damila) from Chola country in South India. There is also no proof of a popular uprising against Elara. On the contrary, both chronicles point out that there was stiff opposition to Dutugamunu from thirty-two chieftains. The *Mahavamsa* even states that there was opposition by his own brothers, Saddha-tissa, and his half brother Dighajantu. This suggests that Elara might well have been a local usurper, not of the Buddhist religion, an infidel, if you like, who had solid support among the local chieftains.

On reading the *Mahavamsa*, it is easy to assume that Buddhism was universally accepted throughout the island from the time of the conversion of Devanampiya-tissa in about 245 BC. While it is likely that there was a considerable uptake of the new religion, there might well have also been large pockets of the population, aristocrat, and commoner alike, who still adhered to their old beliefs. As a matter of fact, even Dutugamunu unwittingly utters the phrase "our family deities," possibly harking back to an older belief of ancestor worship. It should also be noted that the heirs of Devanampiya-tissa lost control of the Anuradhapura Kingdom only a few decades after his death, and Buddhism ceased to enjoy the privileged position it had enjoyed during those earlier years. While the subsequent "foreign" rulers are acknowledged to have governed fairly, they did not confer any special favors on the new religion nor actively support it.

Dutugamunu's family, with its lineage back to Devanampiya-tissa's brothers, Mahanaga and Uttiya, were Buddhists. Many chieftains who opposed him might not have been so and found no great aversion to the likes of Elara, who after all, was a righteous king and possibly even held the same beliefs as themselves. To them, Dutugamunu was nothing more than an impetuous troublesome upstart from the provinces. They had no compelling reason to support him.

If we remove the pejorative "Damila" and the prejudice associated with this word from the *Mahavamsa* text, the story reads more true to form and closely mirrors the *Dipavamsa*:

> A prince named Elara overthrew Asela and ruled justly and respectful of the religion for forty-four years. A prince named Dutugamunu from Ruhunu, with the support of the Sangha, undertook a "holy war" to oust Elara. Dutugamunu faced stiff opposition from thirty-two chieftains and fought many battles on his campaign northward until finally he was victorious. Facing possible defeat, Elara called for reinforcements, but they arrived too late and were routed by Dutugamunu's forces. Dutugamunu cremated Elara according to the Kshatriya code. Dutugamunu then ruled justly and supported the Sangha and built many great monuments, such as the Mirisawetiya and the Ruwanwelisaya.

It is generally agreed that, on the whole, the *Mahavamsa* is a reliable document of history. It never intentionally states a falsehood—but, being an epic poem, it does, on occasion, resort to hyperbole. Written two centuries after the *Dipavamsa* and nearly six centuries after Elara's rule, the narrative appears to be a reflection of the times. A number of invasions from South India and the use of Tamil mercenary soldiers by local rulers, had taken place since the time of Elara, during which time the country had been despoiled. Over time, a wellspring of resentment toward Tamils from South India had developed. It was also a time when Buddhism was on the wane in India and when the first religious schism in Buddhism, sparked by a monk from South India, had occurred. Members of the Buddhist Sangha were genuinely concerned about the fate of their religion and their place in society. Thus the *Mahavamsa*, while maintaining the truthfulness of the main narrative, might have embellished this story, casting Dutugamunu as the champion of the resurgence of Sinhala nationalism and a true defender of Buddhism. The added embellishment of Elara might have been an attempt by the author to restitute him after being vilified as a Damila, a nonbeliever, and make him a worthy adversary to Dutugamunu.

On hearing that Dutugamunu was near death and would not live to see the completion of the project most dear to him—the mighty Ruwanwelisaya—Saddha-tissa, his brother, rushed to Anuradhapura from Dighavapi to the south of the island and personally set about ensuring that his brother would see his project as if completed before his death. Saddha-tissa commandeered the tailors of the city and set them the task of making a massive shroud that they draped over the unfinished dagoba. He then constructed a temporary spire of woven bamboo atop the unfinished structure and covered it, too, with cloth. He then declared to his dying brother that the dagoba was indeed complete.

The *Mahavamsa* relates with great pathos the final moments of the king as he lay on a palanquin and gazed upon his finest creation—the Ruwanwelisaya. Addressing one of the five hundred monks who had journeyed with him on his initial campaign he reflected:

> Formerly, I fought with you, the ten great warriors by my side; now I have entered alone upon the battle with death, and the foe of death is unconquerable.

Salirajakumara, Dutugamunu's son, had fallen in love with a beautiful low-caste maiden named Asokamala. For her love, he forfeited his right to the kingdom. **Saddha-tissa (77–59 BC)**, Dutugamunu's brother, took the reins of government and continued many of the projects commenced by his older brother, including the completion of the mighty Ruwanwelisaya dagoba. During his reign, an accidental fire destroyed magnificent Lovamahapaya. He rebuilt it, albeit to a lesser scale. He built innumerable viharas and dagobas throughout the country and gained much favor with the Sangha for his meritorious work. The Mulkirigala Vihara near Tangalle in southern Sri Lanka, where the *Mahavamsa* Tika was discovered by George Turnour in 1826, was also constructed by him. The kingdom then passed through three of his sons, the last of who was murdered by his army chief.

Ruwanwelisaya, when originally constructed by Dutugamunu in 80 BC, was the largest brick structure in the world. Even today, it is the world's third largest brick structure.

VATTAGAMANI-ABHAYA (44, 29–17 BC)
First "Foreign" Invasion?

Vattagamani-abhaya, a younger son of Saddha-tissa and the nephew of Dutugamunu, swiftly ousted the army chief who had murdered his older brothers and installed himself as monarch. To further legitimize his rule, he took his dead brother's widow as his queen and adopted his dead brother's young son, Mahaculi, as his own.

According to the *Mahavamsa*, in the fifth month of his reign, Vattagamini was confronted by a rebellion from within his kingdom by a Brahmin named Tissa and a serious external threat from seven Tamil chiefs who landed on the west coast of the island with a large militia. Both antagonists sent the king messages demanding that he hand over the royal parasol, the *senachatra*—the symbol of sovereignty. Realizing that he did not have the resources to fight on two fronts, in a wily move, Vattagamini neutralized the internal insurrection by offering the kingdom to the rebels on the condition that they vanquished the Tamils. The insurgents enthusiastically set out to confront the Tamils and were soundly defeated. Having eliminated the internal threat, Vattagamini then marched his army to challenge the advancing Tamils at Kolambahalaka, the same place where Dutugamunu had defeated the relieving army of Bhalluka half a century earlier. In the ensuing battle, Vattagamini's forces were ignominiously defeated. While beating a hasty retreat from the city, the king and his retinue passed the Jain monastery of Tittharama. Seeing the king fleeing, the chief abbot, Nigantha Giri, yelled out derisively at the king, "The great black Sinhala lion is fleeing!" Hugely affronted by this disparaging mockery, the king vowed that when he regained his throne, he would raise a mighty vihara on this very site. To add insult to injury, in his haste to escape, not only did the king jettison his second wife, Somadevi, but he also let fall into the invaders' hands the sacred Alms Bowl of Buddha. Both were promptly carted off to India as war booty.

The foreigners occupied the country for fourteen long years. The first of their rulers was **Pulahattha (43–40 BC)**. He was assassinated by his chief minister **Bahiya (40–38 BC)**, who ruled for two years before he was assassinated by his chief minister **Panayamava (38–31 BC)**. Panayamava, in turn, ruled for seven years before he too met a gruesome end by the hands of his chief minister **Pilayamava (31–30 BC)**, who ruled for a year. **Dathiya (30–29 BC)** deposed Pilayamava and ruled for two years. During the fourteen years of foreign rule, the kingdom was mismanaged by the interlopers, who neglected its vast irrigation systems, the lifeblood of this civilization. Their neglect, together with a catastrophic famine, devastated the kingdom. Without a strong Dharmaraja to guide them, the people cowered under the yoke of foreign subjugation. The social and religious fabric of the land was torn asunder. The people starved, some even resorting to cannibalism. Lawlessness and despondence reigned supreme.

Meanwhile, in exile, Vattagamini befriended a monk named Maha-tissa, who helped him find refuge from his pursuers. For fourteen years, the king hid in the forests, the mountains, and the caves in Dambulla, as well as at temples such as Alu Vihara in Matale, mustering an army strong enough to oust the foreign invaders. In 29 BC, Vattagamini finally defeated the last of the Tamil rulers, Dathiya, and reentered Anuradhapura. One of his first acts on regaining his kingdom was to demolish the Tittharama Jain monastery of Nigantha Giri, and build the mighty Abhayagiri Vihara on its site. The name is said to be derived from the king's name, "Abhaya," and that of his tormentor, "Giri." The building of Abhayagiri marked the end of Brahmin and Jain influence in the country. It also signaled the slow disengagement of ruling monarchs from the Mahavihara. Vattagamini was wary of the monks of the Mahavihara, who had grown accustomed to royal patronage and largess. Upon the completion of the Abhayagiri vihara, he did not, as was customary, donate it to the Mahavihara fraternity. Much to their consternation, he bequeathed the entire complex to his friend and mentor, the monk Maha-tissa. This was the first time that a gift had been made to an individual monk rather than to the fraternity of the Mahavihara. The king also negotiated the return of his second wife, Somadevi. Perhaps out of guilt, or as restitution for having dispensed with her during his flight from the city many years earlier—albeit with her acquiescence—Vattagamini built a monastery at Abhayagiri in her honor (some claim this to be Queen's Pavilion today). On his return to power, Vattagamini set about reenergizing his people by engaging them in massive public works projects. The construction of Abhayagiri and numerous reservoirs might have served a twofold purpose, being both a sign of his thanksgiving for his return to power and a massive public works project designed to address the more serious economic and social malice that afflicted his kingdom.

Here too, an anomaly exists between the *Dipavamsa* and *Mahavamsa*. According to the *Dipavamsa,* five kings ruled for fourteen years, the last of who was a Damila. The *Mahavamsa,* on the other hand, states that all five rulers were Damilas. We cannot ascertain for certain if these rulers were merely non-Buddhist or Tamil invaders from South India.

Three other noteworthy events took place during Vattagamini's reign. The first was the great schism between the dominant Mahavihara and the monks of the new Abhayagiri vihara. At first, the monks of Abhayagiri adhered to the orthodox Theravada doctrine, but they soon grew disenchanted with the opulent, elitist lifestyle of the Mahavihara monks. By contrast, Maha-tissa, the head monk at Abhayagiri, epitomized the simpler, purer virtues of Buddhism. Motivated by jealousy or fear of the loss of royal patronage, the monks of the Mahavihara censured those of the Abhayagiri over a number of seemingly petty transgressions. One such accusation was a charge of associating with commoners. A number of younger monks of the Mahavihara, exasperated by these petty incriminations, abandoned the Mahavihara and joined the Abhayagiri. The king, too, was vexed that the Mahavihara had chastised his chosen monk and had, by association, affronted him. He continued to support the Abhayagiri monks, in defiance of the Mahavihara. In this way, the monks of the Abhayagiri broke away from the Mahavihara, which until then had been the sole custodian of doctrine and theology on the island. Here were sown the seeds of discontent that would manifest themselves in a cataclysmic rupture years later. The second event was the assembly of a synod of monks to put down in writing the three pitakas (baskets of books): the oral traditions of the teachings of the Buddha, the disciplinary rules for monks, and the analysis of Buddhist philosophy. These canons and commentaries (*Atthakatha*), originally written in Pali, were brought to the island by Mahinda and translated into the local vernacular, Sinhala. It was during this time that these works were formally put down in writing. The Sinhala *Atthakatha*, as it came to be known, were the foundation documents for the later *Dipavamsa* and *Mahavamsa*. The third was that Vattagamini might have hastened the decline of other religions on the island and made Buddhism the preeminent religion of the land. Although Vattagamini was no doubt a most illustrious king, the *Mahavamsa*, written by the monks of the Mahavihara, is restrained in its eloquence for this monarch because of his support for Abhayagiri. Had the writings of the Abhayagiri monastery survived, we might well have learned more of Vattagamani-abhaya.

Cora-naga, the wayward son of King Vattagamani-abhaya, was deliberately sidelined by his father in favor of his cousin **Mahaculi Maha-tissa (17 BC–AD 3)** who ascended the throne on King Vattagamani-abhaya's, death.

Anula (AD 9–16)
First Queen, Debaucheress and Her Paramours

Cora-naga (AD 3–9) only attained the throne after his cousin's death. He was an unsavory character indeed. While his real name was Mahanaga, the chronicles refer to him by his nickname, Cora-naga—Naga, the Bandit. His reign was one of oppression and terror. Cora-naga ruled Anuradhapura at about the time when Jesus Christ was born in the faraway land of Palestine.

Twelve years into his reign, Cora-naga was poisoned by his wife, Anula. **Tissa (AD 9–12)**, the eldest son of Mahaculi Maha-tissa, had been just a boy when Cora-naga vested control of the monarchy after his father's death. Now a young man, he moved quickly to thwart any attempts by Anula to seize the throne and quickly installed himself as king. While remaining a member of Tissa's royal household, Anula was besotted by a palace guard named Siva; together, they hatched a dastardly plot. Anula poisoned Tissa and handed the reins of government to **Siva I (AD 12–13),** who, in turn, made Anula his queen. Siva ruled for one year and two months, during which time Anula fell in love with the town architect, a Damila named **Vatuka (AD 13–14).** She poisoned Siva and married Vatuka, who also reigned for a year and two months before Anula poisoned him and married a lower-caste wood carrier named **Darubhatika-tissa (AD 14–15)**. He lasted only one year and one month before being poisoned too. Her next paramour was a Damila Brahmin priest named **Niliya (AD 15–15)**. He was Anula's last consort, reigning for only six months. It seems that thereafter she found it difficult to find any more lovers but is said to have taken her pleasure with "thirty-two of the palace guards." Anula then ruled in her own right for another four months.

Appalled by Anula's debauchery, the populace entreated **Kutakanna-tissa (AD 16–38)**, the second son of Mahaculi Mahatissa, to redeem them from this lecherous queen. Kutakanna-tissa, fearing Anula, had earlier taken refuge in a monastery. Setting aside his priestly robes, Kutakanna-tissa raised an army and marched on the capital. He met very little resistance; Anula's forces readily defected to his side. It is not entirely clear how Anula came to her end, but it appears that she was slain and her palace set ablaze, becoming her funeral pyre.

Ila-naga (AD 93, 95–103)
First Ruler to Employ Tamil Mercenaries

Ila-naga's right to rule—his only claim being descent from the female line of the ruling dynasty—was immediately challenged by members of the Lambakanna clan, who traced their ancestry back to a prince who accompanied the sacred Bodhi tree to the island nearly four hundred and fifty years earlier. This clan had grown extremely powerful and now dared challenge the authority of the king and the Vijayan dynasty that had ruled the land for centuries. Members of the clan deliberately affronted Ila-naga by walking out of the king's coronation ceremony. This was an open display of their contempt for him, and throwing into question the legitimacy of his rule. Ila-naga was outraged and ordered the haughty Lambakannas rounded up, stripped of their lavish garments, and press-ganged into service as lowly coolies—manual laborers. To drive home their disgrace and nettle their pride even further, the king ordered that they be supervised by overseers of the lowest class. The public was highly amused to see the haughty Lambakannas dressed in loincloths doing manual labor. The Lambakannas, on the other hand, did not take their public humiliation lying down; they quickly turned the tables on Ila-naga, capturing him and imprisoning him in his palace. The *Mahavamsa* relates a captivating tale of how Ila-naga's queen dressed their baby son in festive clothes and smuggled a message through him to the royal elephant, which broke out of its stable, stormed the palace, and knocked down its walls. In the ensuing melee, Ila-naga escaped and fled to India. The elephant too absconded into the forests of the Malaya country to await its master's return.

After three years, Ila-naga returned at the head of an army of mercenaries from South India. Landing in Ruhunu, in the south, he mustered support from the Sangha and local sympathizers and waged war on the Lambakannas and regained his throne. The king's vengeance was swift. He beheaded so many of his foes that their bodies lay strewn axle-deep around his chariot. But instead of executing them all, as he had first intended, he was persuaded by his mother to show them mercy. He did so by then meting out a lesser punishment. He had their noses and toes amputated, yoked them to his chariot two by two, and paraded them through the streets of the capital in a triumphal march.

The story of Ila-naga is significant for two reasons. First, he has the distinction of being the first ruler to employ foreign mercenaries from South India, in a local power struggle. It was a stratagem that would be adopted over and over again in the future by contenders to the throne, to the immeasurable detriment of the country. Second, the rise of the Lambakanna clan would, in just a few short years, bring down the Vijayan dynasty that had ruled the kingdom since its founding. From this time on, dynastic and personal rivalries involving this clan would drain the lifeblood from this civilization. These two events would have far-reaching repercussions on the Anuradhapura Kingdom.

YASALAKA-TISSA (AD 112–120)
The Foolhardy Monarch

Yasalaka-tissa usurped the throne by murdering his older brother, Candamukha-siva. This king had a penchant for playing practical jokes, one of which led to his own execution by his gatekeeper. By his own folly Yasalaka-tissa, brought about the end of the House of Vijaya, which had ruled the country for more than six hundred years.

SUBHARAJA (AD 120–127)
The Opportunistic Gatekeeper

Subha was the gatekeeper for the reigning king Yasalaka-tissa, who bore an uncanny resemblance to the monarch. One day Yasalaka-tissa played a practical joke on his ministers by dressing the gatekeeper up as himself while he, in turn, donned the clothes of the gatekeeper. On entering the court, the ministers paid homage to their king—not realizing that, in fact, this was a pretender. On seeing his ruse succeed, King Yasalaka-tissa burst into hysteric laughter. Subha haughtily turned to the ministers and asked curtly, "Why does a lowly gatekeeper behave so insolently in the presence of the monarch?" The foolhardy king, still dressed in his gatekeeper's garb, was hauled away and executed.

Subha, who took on the royal name Subharaja, then set about consolidating his power by eliminating all claimants to the throne. Legend has it that he was greatly disconcerted by a prophecy that "one named Vasabha shall be king." Consumed by fear, Subharaja decreed that every person bearing that name be executed. However, a young boy with that name did survive. Fearful of his imminent demise, Subha had his young daughter, Mahamatta, bundled up together with the royal insignia and spirited out of the palace to safety. He entrusted her care to an old friend, a brick mason who raised the little girl in obscurity as his own daughter.

Vasabha (AD 127–171)
The First Lambakanna King

At the time when King Subharaja decreed that all persons bearing the name "Vasabha" be executed, a boy by that very name was serving under the commander-in-chief of Subharaja's army. The army chief, dutiful to his sovereign, intended to hand over the lad at the earliest opportunity. However, his wife, Pottha, the boy's aunt, was determined to save him. Unable to warn the child beforehand, she devised a plan to spare his life. On the day the commander-in-chief was to visit the palace to hand the boy over, she prepared his betel bag (a chewed concoction with an astringent taste) and intentionally omitted one of the key ingredients, knowing too well that her husband would send for it. As planned, he did, sending young Vasabha to collect it. She warned young Vasabha of the prophecy and the imminent threat to his life, then helped him flee to the Mahavihara, which secretly granted him sanctuary. There he lived in anonymity until one day, he again heard a leper's prophecy that he would be king. Inspired, Vasabha set out to oust the usurper king, Subharaja.

Although not of royal birth, as a member of the powerful Lambakanna clan Vasabha, did not have much difficulty raising an army to confront Subharaja. Moreover, with the Vijayan dynasty extinguished, the path was open for a popular aspirant with a reasonable pedigree to vest control of the government. Vasabha made Pottha, his now widowed aunt who saved his life, his principal queen, and firmly established the Lambakannas as the second dynasty to rule the Anuradhapura Kingdom.

Besides ordering the construction of numerous religious buildings and irrigation projects, Vasabha also raised the city wall and fortified the main gates with fortress towers. It is not known why he felt these precautions necessary, unless the foreign incursion referred to during the time of his successor actually took place during his reign, and he felt it prudent to bolster his defenses. Inscriptions attributed to him found throughout the island confirm that his authority extended over the entire island.

Vankanasika-tissa (AD 171–174)
The King Who Married a Commoner

As already mentioned, Subharaja had a lovely young daughter named Mahamatta, who had been spirited away from the palace at the time of her father's ouster and placed in the care of a brick mason. There she lived in anonymity. When King Vasabha was in search of a suitable bride for his heir apparent, he consulted the palace soothsayer, who advised the king to seek out a young girl—the daughter of a bricklayer. The king dutifully followed the soothsayer's advice, and Mahamatta's true identity was discovered. As foretold, the king's son, Vankanasika-tissa, married the beautiful Mahamatta. This is the only recorded instance in which a queen was not of the same social class as the king. Mahamatta may have been the exception because of her extreme beauty or, as is most likely the case, because she was considered sufficiently "royal," having been born during Subharaja's tenure as king when he married Mahamatta's mother, who might have been of noble descent.

The *Pujavali*, written in the seventeenth century, records an incursion into Lanka by South Indians during the reign of this monarch. The foreign invaders are said to have captured twelve thousand Sinhalese and taken them back to South India. There they were used as slaves in the construction of embankments of the Kaveri River. It is possible that this event took place, but the number of captives is probably grossly exaggerated, there being no mention of this event in the *Dipavamsa* or *Mahavamsa*.

Wheel thrown, low fired 55cm tall storage jar with paddle impressions over the exterior surface; primarily for storing water and goods. (circa 1-2 century).

Gajabahu I (AD 174–196)
First King to Visit a Foreign Land

Gajabahu's personal name was Gamini Abhaya, but he is known by the sobriquet Gajabahu—he whose arm has the strength of an elephant —which suggests that he had military exploits to his credit. The son of Vankanasika-tissa and Mahamatta, Gajabahu enjoys a special place in the modern Sinhala psyche. While the *Dipavamsa* and *Mahavamsa* are scant in their accounts of his activities, mentioning only his monastic building projects, the *Pujavali* and *Rājāvaliya* provide vivid accounts of his exploits in India. It is probably these latter accounts that form the basis for the esteem in which he is held by Sinhalese today.

According to the *Rājāvaliya*, this king had a habit of disguising himself as a commoner and walking incognito though his capital to learn firsthand about the well-being of his citizens. One night while on his rounds, the king heard the pitiful wails of a woman weeping and thought to himself, "some wrong has been done in this city." Marking the door of her dwelling with a piece of chalk, the king returned to his palace. The following morning he inquired of his ministers if they knew of any injustices done in the city to which they replied, "O great king, it is like a wedding house." The king was displeased by their response and sent for the woman who explained that her two sons were among the twelve thousand kidnapped and taken captive to India. Gajabahu, who knew nothing of this large-scale abduction, immediately launched a campaign to retrieve them. Arriving at his point of embarkation, he had a change of heart, dismissed his army, and accompanied by his favorite giant [bodyguard] named Nila, Gajabahu set out for India alone. Together they overawed the Chola king with their physical prowess and guile and befriended him. Gajabahu returned not only with those Sinhalese taken captive but also, as recompense, twelve thousand men from the Chola Kingdom. Sinhala ballads and the *Rājāvaliya* also state that Gajabahu brought back the anklet of Pattini on his return from India.

One could easily dismiss this story as fable if not for the South Indian epic *Silappatikaram* (The Tale of an Anklet) written in the second century, which contains the tale of Kannagi, a woman who lost her husband through a miscarriage of justice in the Pandyan court and took vengeance on the kingdom. She was later deified as Pattini. Gajabahu is said to have been present at the consecration of a shrine to Pattini by King Vel Kelu Kuttuvan, also known as Kadal Pirakottiya Senguttuvan Chera.

The relevant passage in the *Silappatikaram* 30th Canto, 160 reads:

> The monarch of the world circumambulated the shrine thrice and stood professing his respects. In front of him the Arya [Kalinga] kings released from prison, kings removed from the central jail, the Kongu ruler of Kudagu [Karnataka], the king of Malva [west-central northern India] and *Kayavaku, the king of sea-girt Lanka*, prayed reverently to the deity thus…

It is plausible that Senguttuvan Chera, the ruler of the Chera Kingdom in South India, who had recently placed a kinsman of his on the throne of Chola Kingdom, was magnanimous toward his friend Gajabahu. He redressed Gajabahu's grievances against the Cholas by not only returning Gajabahu's subjects but also giving him an equal number of Chola prisoners as recompense. Gajabahu returned home triumphant.

Pattini, an important deity among Buddhist and Hindus of Lanka.

The fact that only scant mention is made of Gajabahu in the *Dipavamsa* and *Mahavamsa* was, it seems, an omission of an inconvenient truth. Gajabahu is associated with the introduction of the goddess Pattini. The orthodox Mahavihara would have looked upon the introduction of an alien goddess into the pantheon of local deities with great alarm tantamount to heresy. Hence the *Dipavamsa* and *Mahavamsa* chose to conveniently ignore the whole episode. Since the story of Elara appears to have been partly derived from the *Silappatikaram*, it would be odd indeed for the author of the *Mahavamsa* to have been unfamiliar with the rest of the work, including its reference to Gajabahu. Finally, although Gajabahu did build many monastic establishments, he was one of the most generous patrons of the Abhayagiri vihara, which he enlarged—another activity that would have been viewed with disdain by the monks of the Mahavihara.

The Alms Bowl of Buddha and the Anklet of Pattini, if they were ever brought back from India by Gajabahu, have long since disappeared. Gajabahu's legacy is the introduction of the deity Pattini and the "Gajabahu Synchronism."

The *Gajabahu Synchronism* is used by historians to date early South Indian Tamil literature, for no Tamil records can be used for accurate chronological purposes. The reign of Gajabahu is known (AD 174–196). The association between Gajabahu and King Senguttuvan Chera makes the latter his contemporary, thus providing a useful reference date from which to date Tamil literature. Gajabahu died without an heir, and the kingdom passed to his brother-in-law, a powerful member of the Lambakanna clan.

VIJAYA-KUMARA (AD 302–303)
The Rise of the Three Brothers

Vijaya-kumara, on ascending the throne, summoned three princes named Samgha-tissa, Samghabohi, and Gothabhaya, who were possibly half-brothers of the king, to assist him in the administration of the kingdom. While walking to the capital, the three brothers passed a blind man seated by the side of the road. On hearing their footsteps, he prophesied: "The ground bears here three rulers of the earth!" Gothabhaya, who was walking last, heard this, stopped, and asked what his pronouncement meant, but the blind man refused to elaborate. His curiosity aroused, Gothabhaya then asked, "Whose race will endure?" to which the blind man replied, "That of the last." Gothabhaya fell silent and joined his brothers. He did not reveal this conversation to his companions. On their arrival at the palace, the king appointed each to high office. Gothabhaya, anxious to realize the blind man's prophecy, soon sought to hasten his own ascension: he conspired with the most senior of the princes, Samgha-tissa, and murdered the king.

SAMGHA-TISSA (AD 303–307)
Poisoned for His Love of Jambu Fruits

Samgha-tissa had a weakness for jambu fruit. This fruit is not the jambu fruit known today, but rather a grape-like fruit having an astringent taste that originated in Jambudvipa (India). Samgha-tissa, together with his harem and the royal court, frequently journeyed to Pachinadipaka, where the best fruit grew. The local villagers soon tired of the king's frequent visits, which drained their meager resources when they were forced to entertain him. Finally, in exasperation, they poisoned the fruits of the king's favorite jambu tree. He came, he ate, and he died.

Samghabohi (AD 307–309)
The Saintly King

Gothabhaya then convinced the next senior prince, Samghabohi, to take up kingship. Samghabohi was a very pious man with little interest in the kingship, and it was with great trepidation that he accepted. Power did not corrupt Samghabohi, who was a strict adherent of the Five Precepts (do not kill living things, refrain from taking the property of others, do not commit adultery, avoid lying, and do not drink intoxicating beverages). To him, his religious convictions took precedence over all else. Life was so sacrosanct to him that when some rebels rose up against him, rather than executing them for treason, he secretly released them, and substituted cadavers of naturally deceased people in their place to create the illusion that he meted out harsh justice. With this gesture, he nullified their opposition to him. When a drought visited the land, he fasted and prayed until the rains were restored. When a pestilence beset the populace, he offered his own life to alleviate it. His subjects came to believe that it was by Samghabohi's intercession that these disasters were averted. Gothabhaya found the situation intolerable. Samghabohi's popularity stood in the way of his own prophesied kingship. Anxious to become king, Gothabhaya threatened to revolt, knowing all too well that the king would abdicate rather than cause bloodshed. Samghabohi, as expected, relinquished the throne. Taking only his water-strainer (a device to remove tiny creatures and purify water, which was one of the requisites of an ascetic monk), he clandestinely left the city and withdrew into the life of a recluse. In his solitude, Samghabohi found contentment. Gothabhaya, on the other hand, wished his brother dead. He resented and dreaded the deposed king's popularity. He knew all too well, however, that any direct action against Samghabohi would result in open revolt. Gothabhaya roiled in silent indignation. One day, Samghabohi happened upon a poor man who, although so poor, insisted on sharing his meager meal with this enigmatic hermit. The ex-king was deeply moved by the man's generosity and said to him, "I am King Samghabohi; take thou my head and show it to Gothabhaya, for he will give thee much gold." The man vehemently refused to do any such thing, and the king, to render him a service, gave up the ghost and died on the spot. Glad that he had no hand in his demise, Gothabhaya was overjoyed when presented with Samghabohi's head and rewarded the man generously. He then respectfully carried out the funeral rites for Samghabohi, some say at Isurumuniya. Revered today as Siri-Samghabohi, he is seen as the embodiment of selflessness and epitomized the ideals of enlightened Buddhist kingship.

Gothabhaya (AD 309–322)
The Rise of Religious Discontent

Having snatched the throne from the saintly Samghabohi, Gothabhaya spent lavishly to gain the goodwill of the Sangha and the people. To further win favor with the monks of the Mahavihara, Gothabhaya instigated a pogrom against the monks of Abhayagiri, who were adherents of the Mahayanan doctrine and were viewed with hostility by the more orthodox Mahavihara. Gothabhaya went so far as to banish sixty of them from his kingdom, some say after branding them with hot irons. They fled to southern India, where an Indian monk named Samghhamitta took up their cause, came to Lanka, and took up residence at Abhayagiri, where he fomented further discontent over dogma. In a great conclave held at the Thuparama monastery, Samghhamitta held sway and convinced Gothabhaya to look favorably on his doctrine. There was much consternation among the monks of the Mahavihara at this outright blasphemy: the king had sided with the doctrine of a foreign heretic.

Gothabhaya was so taken with Samghhamitta that he entrusted the education of his two young sons, Jettha-tissa and Mahasena, to the monk. Jettha-tissa, the older, developed an early dislike for the monk. Mahasena, the younger, was more malleable and took to the monk's teachings. Gothabhaya earned much antipathy during his reign, first because of his persecution of the monks of the Abhayagiri monastery and then because of his support of the heretical teaching of Samghhamitta.

Jettha-Tissa I (AD 323–334)
The Cruel

Jettha-tissa succeeded his father Gothabhaya and earned the nickname "The Cruel" for the punishment he meted out to sixty nobles who had expressed their displeasure at the dead king's persecution of the monks of the Abhayagiri and his support of the heretic Samghhamitta. When these nobles refused to take part in his father's funeral procession, Jettha-tissa rounded them up and had them impaled on stakes around his father's funeral pyre.

Jettha-tissa was no friend of the monk Samghhamitta. Fearing for his life, Samghhamitta fled to India. Jettha-tissa supported the Mahavihara and carried out many meritorious acts in the hope of mitigating his misdeeds.

Impalement similar to that meted out by Jettha-tissa, circa 15th century imprint

MAHASENA (AD 334–362)
The Repentant Heretic

Mahasena succeeded his brother Jettha-tissa. His first act upon ascending the throne was to summon Samghhamitta back from India to officiate at his coronation. This was the first time since the introduction of Buddhism that the chief monk of the Mahavihara had not officiated. The signs were ominous for the Mahavihara.

Samghhamitta had the king's ear, and one fateful morning the beating of drums announced a royal proclamation: "whoever gives food to the bhikkhu dwelling in the Mahavihara is liable to a fine of one hundred coins." For three days, the monks of the Mahavihara came with their begging bowls but returned empty-handed for not a soul dared to defy the king. Soon the occupants of the Mahavihara faced the serious prospect of starvation, but the monks were resolute. They would not compromise their cherished Theravada doctrine in favor of the new Mahayana doctrine of the king and his priestly cohort. Driven by hunger and deprivation, the monks slowly abandoned the monasteries of the Mahavihara and fled into the hinterlands of Malaya and Ruhunu. "Ownerless land belongs to the king," Samghhamitta counseled, so, gaining the king's acquiescence, he set about the dismemberment of the vast property of the Mahavihara. Buildings and treasure accumulated over a thousand years from donations by pious kings and commoners alike were pilfered and transported to Abhayagiri. Even the magnificent Lovamahapaya, only recently renovated by Jettha-tissa, was dismantled and its contents used to enrich the Abhayagiri monastery. Abhayagiri gained handsomely from the misfortunes of the Mahavihara, and, to their discredit, the monks of this monastery remained shamefully silent—and were even complicit in this wanton destruction. With the acquisition of the spoils of the Mahavihara and the king's support, Abhayagiri was soon the preeminent Buddhist institution of the land and would remain so for centuries to come.

All did not bode well for Mahasena. Slowly opposition coalesced around Meghavannabhaya, the king's closest friend, who, on seeing the unholy destruction around him, abandoned the king, fled to Malaya, and assembled a large army to confront Mahasena. Gathering strength through Ruhunu, he marched on the capital. The king, in turn, also set forth to do battle.

While preparing for his evening meal, Meghavannabhaya came across a special delicacy that he knew his old friend, the king, would relish. In a gesture of camaraderie, he sneaked into the king's camp, where he was soon recognized and taken directly to Mahasena The king, who had always held his friend in high esteem, was pleased to see him, and together they shared the food Meghavannabhaya had brought with him. When the king had eaten, he looked up and inquired, "Why hast thou become a rebel?" Meghavannabhaya replied, "Because the Mahavihara has been destroyed by thee." Mahasena reflected on this for a long while, then replied: "I will make the vihara to be dwelt in yet again; forgive my fault." Through this reconciliation, a battle was averted. The king returned to the capital, and Meghavannabhaya set out to rebuild the Mahavihara. Meanwhile, Samghhamitta, on his way to destroy Thuparama monastery, came to grief when a laborer employed by one of the king's wives assassinated him.

The king then befriended a monk named Tissa from the Dakkhinarama vihara, where a breakaway group of monks from the Abhayagiri known as the Sagalika sect had taken up residence and formed their own cell. They, too, were not in favor with the Mahavihara because of their unconventional views. Tissa convinced the king to build a new monastery on a large tract of land known as the Jotivana Gardens, south of the city. Once known as the Nandana Park, these were the very gardens where Mahinda had preached to the multitudes nearly six hundred years earlier. Claiming that the land was unoccupied, Mahasena requisitioned it and constructed the largest dagoba ever built, and even today the largest brick structure in the world, dwarfing all the dagobas of the Mahavihara and Abhayagiri. (The *Mahavamsa* describes this massive edifice in just two verses.) He then installed Tissa as the head monk of this new vihara. This establishment came to be known as Jetavana.

Despite the religious turmoil and near civil war, Mahasena heralded an era of prodigious achievements. Besides restoring parts of the Mahavihara and building the Jetavana, he built and repaired countless other religious establishments and sixteen massive reservoirs, the largest of them Minneriya Tank. Some say that the village folk to whom he provided water from these tanks deified him as "Minneri Deyyo," and he is still worshipped today at a shrine near Minneriya Tank. The era of gigantic dagobas and monasteries ended with the death of Mahasena.

The most significant event to take place during his reign was the writing of the *Dipavamsa*, the first chronicle of the island's history. Written by the monks of the Mahavihara during their nine years of diaspora, it was an attempt to record their legacy, which they truly felt was near extinction.

The *Dipavamsa* and the *Mahavamsa* end with the death of this monarch.

SIRIMEGHAVANNA (AD 362–390)
First King of the Culavamsa

Sirimeghavanna, the son of Mahasena, was the first king of the *Culavamsa* or Lesser Chronicle. He spent most of his reign repairing the damage inflicted on the Mahavihara by his late father.

Sirimeghavanna was a contemporary of the Indian emperor Samuddragupta (AD 345-380). According to the Chinese source Hing-tchoan of Wang Hiuen-tse, two devotees on a pilgrimage to the sacred Bodhi tree in India reported to the king of the lack of accommodations there for pilgrims. Sirimeghavanna (the Chinese refered to him as Ch-mi-kia-po-ma) sent an embassy with presents to emperor Samuddragupta and received permission to build a monastery there. An inscription recently discovered on the site appears to confirm this.

The most noteworthy event of his reign was the arrival of the Tooth Relic of the Buddha. It was brought to Anuradhapura for safekeeping by the daughter of the king of Kalinga, disguised as a Brahmin woman. Sirimeghavanna built a temple to house this relic and ordered that an annual festival be held, during which it was taken in procession to the Abhayagiri dagoba for public veneration.

Early 20th century painting depicting Princess Hemamala smuggling the tooth relic to Lanka hidden in her hair.

The tooth relic is said to be the left canine tooth of the Buddha. Over time, a belief grew that whoever possessed this relic had a divine right to rule. Many rulers in India had vied to have it in their possession, and non-Buddhists sought just as ardently to destroy it. For this reason, it was secreted away to Lanka, where it has remained ever since.

MAHANAMA (AD 409–431)
The Licentious Monk Who Became a Righteous King

Mahanama was a monk and also the younger brother of the reigning monarch Upa-tissa I (AD unknown–409). He was having an illicit love affair with the queen, who killed the king by stabbing him while they were in a "quiet place" to make way for her lover. On attaining the throne, Mahanama married her. The most important historic event to take place during his rule was the translation back into Pali of the Sinhala Tripitaka (baskets of books) and Atthakatha commentaries written during the reign of Vattagamani-abhaya nearly five hundred years earlier. Acariya Buddhaghosa, a learned Brahmin who had converted to Buddhism, was specially engaged for this purpose. The Culavamsa notes that at the time when Buddhaghosa undertook his task, the original Pali Atthakatha had disappeared in India. Ironically, the Sinhala Atthakatha has since been lost as well. Some have suggested that they were destroyed as irrelevant after Buddhaghosa had completed his work. Only Buddhaghosa's Pali translation of these documents exists today, and it is a basis for the clarification of many important points of Buddhist philosophy.

It was also during the reign of this monarch that Faxian, a Chinese chronicler monk, visited Anuradhapura in AD 411, staying at the Abhayagiri vihara for two years. He provides us with the first independent insight into the kingdom. He wrote:

> In the city there are many Vaisya [Indian] and Sabaean [Arab] merchants whose houses are stately and beautiful. The lanes and passages are kept in good order. At the heads of four principle streets they have built preaching halls where, on the eighth, fourteenth, and fifteenth days of the month, they spread carpets and set forth a pulpit, while the monks and commonalty from all quarters come together to hear the law. The people say that in the kingdom there may be altogether sixty thousand monks, who get their food from their common stores. The king, besides, prepares elsewhere in the city a common supply of food for five or six thousand more. When any want, take as much as the vessels will hold, all returning with them full.

Mahanama had no heirs, and with his death the first Lambakanna dynasty, founded by Vasabha three centuries earlier, floundered and effectively came to an end. The leaders who followed him were weak and lacked the moral authority to govern the kingdom. The ensuing leadership vacuum paved the way for foreign adventurers to exploit the situation.

Faxian (also known as Fa-hsien) was a Chinese Buddhist monk who travelled by foot from China to Lanka, visiting many sacred Buddhist sites. He spent 2 years at the Abhayagiri monastery.

SOTTHI-SENA TO MITTA-SENA (AD 431–433)
The End of a Dynasty

Sotthi-sena (AD 431–431) was Mahanama's son born of a Damila (foreign) consort. As he was not born to a queen, he had no legitimate claim to the throne. Samgha, Mahanama's daughter by a queen, murdered him that very same afternoon and immediately ceded the kingdom to her husband **Chattaggahaka (AD 431–432)**. Since there appeared to have been no legitimate heir to the throne, there was no opposition to his rise to this role. He died within a year. On his death, his chief minister had his body secretly cremated within the premises of the royal palace and installed a puppet king named **Mitta-sena (AD 432–433)**. According to the *Culavamsa*, Mitta-sena was a rice thief, probably a rice trader. On the pretext that the king was ill, the minister kept Mitta-sena locked away in the palace and wielded power himself.

PANDU TO PITHIYA (AD 433–460)
The Rule of the Five Tamils

Sensing an opportunity, a Tamil leader from South India named Pandu invaded the island and easily defeated Mitta-sena's army and slew Mitta-sena. The origin of the south Indian invasion is not clear. It has been suggested that since their leader is referred to as Pandu, he may, in fact, have been from Pandya. At about this time, South India was ruled by the Kalabhra dynasty, which held sway over the Pandyas, Cholas, and Cheras. Perhaps the invasion from South India was a consequence of the displacement of Pandyans from their homelands during these disturbances.

Pandu and his henchmen Parinda, Khuddaparinda, Tiritara, Dathiya, and Pithiya collectively ruled for twenty-seven years. Although the *Culavamsa* is vague about the degree of their conquest, suggesting that the nobility of Anuradhapura fled to Ruhunu which remained independent, inscriptional evidence as far south as Kataragama, near Ruhunu, suggests that the invaders may at various times have controlled the entire island. Further inscriptional evidence even indicates that these foreign rulers were patrons of Buddhism, making numerous donations to Buddhist religious establishments. It is possible that even though they were not adherents of Buddhism, they found it politically expedient to be seen as supporting the religion of their subjects.

Dhatusena (AD 460–478)
The Instigator of the Mahavamsa

Dhatusena was a member of the Moriya clan that had fled Anuradhapura many generations earlier "for fear of the gatekeeper Subha" (Subharaja). It may well have been that one of their ancestors was named Vasabha. Unbeknownst to the Tamil overlords ruling the kingdom, the young Dhatusena was being tutored for the priesthood at the Mahavihara by his uncle, the monk Mahanama. At a very young age, good omens foretold great things for the young Dhatusena, and it wasn't long before Pandu, the Tamil ruler, got wind of this and attempted to assassinate him. Fearing further assassination attempts, Mahanama fled with his young protégé deep into the forests, where for many years, master and pupil lived a nomadic existence. On coming of age, Dhatusena discarded the saffron robes of a novice monk, donned the garb of a soldier, and undertook a grueling guerrilla campaign to rid his country of the foreign interlopers. One after another, he slew their leaders, but the invaders held on tenaciously, quickly replacing one fallen leader with another, denying Dhatusena a speedy triumph. Finally, in about the tenth year of his campaign, he was victorious and restored Sinhala hegemony over the entire island. Dhatusena, having rid the land of the enemy, applied himself to peace as diligently as he had to war.

Dhatusena had two sons. Kasyapa, the older, was born of a liaison between Dhatusena and "a woman of unequal birth" during his years as a guerrilla fighter. Moggallana, however, although much younger, was born of a queen and thus was the rightful heir to the throne. The *Culavamsa* tells us that the king also had a daughter who was as "dear to him as his own life." She was married to his nephew, Migara, the son of his sister. Dhatusena himself had appointed Migara as commander-in-chief of his army. We are told that Migara "caused her to be flogged on the thighs with a whip although she had committed no offense." She fled to her father. The king, seeing his daughter's garments trickling with blood, was outraged. In an uncontrollable fit of rage, he had Migara's mother, his own sister, stripped naked and burned alive in retribution. Deeply aggrieved by the gruesome death of his mother, Migara conspired with Kasyapa to vest control of the government. Still vengeful and seeking even more revenge, Migara convinced Kasyapa that the old king was hiding a large treasure for Moggallana. Agitated by Migara's constant haranguing, Kasyapa sent messages to his father, demanding the treasure. The stubborn old man, however, remained silent. With each rebuke, Kasyapa's anger grew more intense, and his demands shriller. Finally, Dhatusena, acknowledging his impending death, resolved to visit his mentor and friend Mahanama, purify himself in the waters of the mighty Kala Wewa reservoir, which he himself had constructed, and then resign himself to his fate. Appearing to relent, Dhatusena sent word that he was ready to point out the place where the treasure was concealed, and he asked to be taken to the banks of the Kala Wewa fifty kilometers away. Kasyapa gladly agreed and, intent on amplifying the old king's humiliation, provided him with a "chariot with a bent axle." Dhatusena bathed himself in the Kala Wewa and, emerging from the water purified, pointed to his friend the monk and then, slowly, made a sweeping motion at the shimmering expanse of water before him and said, "O friends, this is all the treasure that I possess!" On learning of this, Kasyapa flew into a rage and ordered Migara, "slay my father." With relish, Migara extacted his revenge. He had Dhatusena stripped naked, bound him in heavy chains, fettered him in a niche of his prison cell, and slowly entombed him alive by plastering up the opening with clay.

Dhatusena's greatest contribution to posterity was his decision to set aside a thousand coins for the reinterpretations of the *Dipavamsa*, the first chronicle of the land. He entrusted this daunting task to his uncle Mahanama, a monk fluent in Pali verse and prose. The outcome of this endeavor was the *Mahavamsa*, the world's oldest and most comprehensive authenticated metrical chronicle of history. It appears that Mahanama's brief was clear: rewrite the *Dipavamsa* to make it comprehensive and eloquent. The *Mahavamsa*, like the *Dipavamsa*, concludes with the death of Mahasena a century earlier. This has led some modern scholars to suggest that Mahanama's brief did not extend to updating the chronology to his time.

The Avukana Buddha statue on the banks of the Kala Wewa was commissioned by Dhatusena. It is possible that the monk Mahanama resided at a vihara here. (circa 5th century).

KASYAPA I (AD 478–496)
Builder of Sigiriya

Kasyapa, the eldest son of King Dhatusena, had his father murdered and usurped the throne. To further consolidate his power, he also attempted to assassinate his younger brother Moggallana, the rightful heir, who fled to India. Resentful of the murder of his father, he undertook many meritorious acts as atonement, but these failed to assuage the clergy or the people. Growing fretful, he abandoned Anuradhapura and built a new capital seventy kilometers farther inland at Sigiriya, an area dominated by a giant granite monolith two hundred meters tall. Atop this massive rock, he built a lavish palace accessible only by way of a narrow perpendicular staircase that wound up the cliff face. In the eighteenth year of his reign, Migara fell out with Kasyapa and secretly switched his allegiance to Moggallana. On hearing of this news, Moggallana returned from India with a motley collection of friends that the *Mahavamsa* euphemistically refers to as his "twelve distinguished friends." Ignoring the dire advice of his soothsayers, who predicted disaster, Kasyapa abandoned the safety of Sigiriya and confronted his brother on the plains below. Mounted on his war elephant, Kasyapa led the charge. Seeing a swamp ahead of him, he turned his elephant to seek an alternate route, but at that very moment, Migara defected to the other side. The army broke and fled. Kasyapa, alone and forsaken but flamboyant to the very end, drew out his dagger, slashed his throat, raised the blade high in the air, sheathed it again, and fell dead. In recognition of his dead brother's gallant act, Moggallana cremated him with honor.

The *Culavamsa* is scant in its description of Kasyapa, summing up his life thus:

> He betook himself through fear to Sihagiri which is difficult to ascent for human beings. He cleared roundabout, surrounded it with a wall and built a staircase in the form of a lion...then he built there a fine palace, worthy to behold, like another Alakamanda, and dwelt there like [the god] Kuvera.

Sigiriya and its beautiful frescoes are Kasyapa's greatest legacy. He also undertook a major reconstruction of the Issarasamana and Vessagiri viharas, renaming them "Isuramenu-Bo-Upulvan-Kasubgiri." in honor of himself and his two daughters. The Isurumuniya Lovers and the sculpture of a royal family found there might have been commissioned by him.

Kasyapa was the last memorable king of the Anuradhapura Kingdom.

The Sigiriya Frescoes painted in AD 483 are one of the finest examples of ancient art. There were over 500 of these painted on a massive panel of over 200 sq m on the side of Sigiriya rock.

AGE OF ANARCHY

The Anuradhapura Kingdom had now lasted nearly a thousand years, reaching its zenith during the time of Dhatusena and his son Kasyapa. Dhatusena was the instigator of the *Mahavamsa*, one of the greatest historical records of the ancient world. Kasyapa's masterpiece, Sigiriya, was an architectural and artistic gem and the last colossal building project undertaken by the people of the Anuradhapura Kingdom

Moggallana, who succeeded Kasyapa, and those that followed him were most renowned for their piety, interdynastic rivalries, and succession disputes. These contenders squandered the resources of the kingdom for their own edification. Their most damaging folly was the introduction of Tamil mercenaries from South India in local dynastic power struggles.

In the final years of the age of anarchy, the country suffered a series of devastating civil wars in which rival claimants to the throne, each seeking an advantage over the other, bolstered the number of their troops by importing more and more foreign mercenaries from the Tamil lands of South India. These Tamil fighters were neither sent back nor absorbed into the local population. Separated by differences of religion, language, customs, and ethnicity, these mercenaries and their descendants developed into a fifth column whose members readily sided with other Tamils in local conflicts. Not only did these newcomers play a part in court intrigues, but they also actively solicited support from Tamil rulers in India, further inflaming already volatile local situations. This Tamil influence became more and more pervasive as rival contenders vied for supremacy.

There is little doubt that this political instability resulted in poor governance, which devastated the economy. This was further exacerbated by many instances of gross ineptitude and the lack of vision by the kings of this period. During the age of anarchy, eighteen rulers reigned in Anuradhapura. Of these, three committed suicide, five were murdered, two fled, and two died in battle. Only eight died of natural causes. Devastated by plundering and the decline of religiosity by the people, the three fraternities too lost power and influence.

A once harmonious community was replaced by one in which two distinct groups lived in mistrust of one another. The kingdom's cohesion was corroding away.

MOGGALLANA I TO SIVA II (AD 496–522)
Harbingers of Decline

Moggallana I (AD 496–513) stripped Sigiriya of its treasures, handed the magnificent complex to the Dhammaruci sect of the Abhayagiri monastery, and returned to Anuradhapura. He meted out rough justice to those who had supported Kasyapa. Gnashing his teeth with rage, he executed more than a thousand of them. Lesser transgressors had their ears and noses cut off and were banished. The *Culavamsa* notes that he acquired the nickname Kakkhasa, a term used to depict the devil. This has led to speculation that he may have had protruding front teeth that he gnashed when angry. His wrath thus spent, he ingratiated himself with the clergy by his acts of piety, which included the renovation of the Ruwanwelisaya and other religious establishments that had been neglected by his predecessor. Also cognizant of the threat of seaborne attack from India, a tactic he himself had employed, Moggallana was the first monarch to set up a coast guard. Migara continued to enjoy the support of the new king and vanished from history during this period. Mahanama, the author of the *Mahavamsa*, also disappeared from history at about this time.

The most notable event during Moggallana's reign was the arrival of the Hair Relic of Buddha, which was brought over from India by one of his kinsmen who had also fled during the reign of Kasyapa.

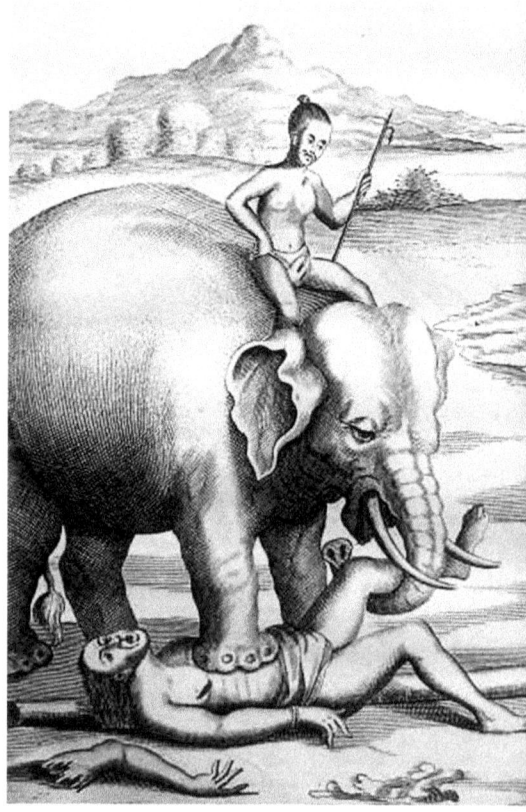

A punishment such as this might have been meted out by Moggallana to Kasyapa's supporters

Kumara-dhatusena (513–522 AD) succeeded his father Moggallana. A scholarly king, he is said to have committed suicide by jumping into the funeral pyre of his favorite poet - Kalidasa. **Kitti-sena (522–522 AD)**, Kumara-dhatusena's son and the last of the Moriyan kings, ruled for a mere nine months before he was murdered by his maternal uncle, who ruled for just twenty-five days as **Siva II (522 –522 AD),** before he too was murdered.

Silameghavanna (AD 617–626)
Emergence of Tamil Influence

Silameghavanna, on becoming king, undertook many meritorious deeds and won the hearts of the people with his kindness and generosity. A disaffected general named Sirinaga, a henchman of his uncle of Jetthatissa, a pretender to the throne, departed for India and soon returned with a large contingent of Tamil mercenaries and captured Uttaradesa, the northern province of the kingdom. The king immediately took the fight to Sirinaga, trounced him convincingly, subjected his captives to all kinds of humiliation, and then consigned the survivors into slavery. Silameghavanna returned to the capital once more and continued his good deeds. About this time, a young monk named Bodhi visited the king and beseeched him to reform the Sangha at the Abhayagiri vihara. The king did so by expelling the wayward monks, who retaliated by killing Bodhi. On hearing of this, the king flew into a rage and had the scoundrels rounded up, and as punishment he had their hands cut off and shackled in chains, he made them the caretakers of the public baths. It was a clear message to all: whatever their station in life, the king was not to be trifled with. Having expelled the unworthy monks of the Abhayagiri vihara, he also commanded that the monks of the Mahavihara carry out common ceremonies with them. The monks of the Mahavihara refused. Silameghavanna died of an unknown disease while visiting Dakkhinadesa province shortly thereafter. The *Culavamsa* hints that his illness was retribution for his attempt to reconcile the ceremonies of the two fraternities.

The reign of Silameghavanna is noteworthy in the story of Anuradhapura because it was during his reign we first hear of large scale involvement of foreigners in local conflicts. Although the battle was a decisive victory for the Sinhalese, it was a precursor of things to come, for the introduction of Tamil mercenaries into local conflicts was to play a crucial role in future battles between local aspirants for the throne. Over time this would contribute to the destabilization of the kingdom and its final demise.

The dynasty that Silameghavanna founded survived until the collapse of the Anuradhapura Kingdom four centuries later.

AGGABODHI III TO HATTHADATHA (AD 626–677)
The Growth of Tamil Influence and Power

Aggabodhi III (AD 626—641), the son of Silameghavanna, was young and inexperienced when he ascended the throne. He was immediately confronted by Jettha-tissa, a rival to the throne, who had previously tried to wrest the kingdom from his father. When Jettha-tissa sent a minister named Dathasiva to threaten territories to the west of the capital, the king mounted an attack and captured Dathasiva. Emboldened by his victory, the young Aggabodhi thought to himself, "one can kill the fellow like a young bird in the nest" and boldly chased Jettha-tissa farther inland, but his forces were soundly defeated. Aggabodhi fled the scene in panic. Ignominiously discarding his royal robes and disguising himself, he hastily set sail for India, abandoning his wealth, country, and kinfolk. **Jettha-tissa (AD 626–626)** finally fulfilled his life's ambition and was now king. But his reign was a short one. Aggabodhi soon returned from India at the head of a mercenary force and joined his supporters in the campaign against Jettha-tissa. The tide quickly turned against Jettha-tissa, and he gallantly committed suicide on the battlefield. He was king for just five months.

Aggabodhi III was restored to the throne just before an interesting incident took place. The *Culavamsa* tells us that "court officials of the King slew the king's brother, Mana", his most trusted lieutenant, confidant and heir apparent. It appears that the king had given his brother permission to enjoy the pleasures of the royal harem, but the guards unwittingly killed him, thinking him an intruder. On hearing of the loss of a great general, Dathasiva, who had been biding his time in India since the death of Jettha-tissa, returned at the head of another mercenary Tamil army and routed the king's forces. Aggabodhi again fled to India, taking only the "pearl chain of one string", a symbol of office, with him as proof of his royal identity.

Dathopa-tissa I (AD 641–652) was the name Dathasiva adopted on proclaiming himself king. It wasn't long before Aggabodhi returned with another foreign army and seized power once more. For the next five years, their fight swung this way and that, and the whole country suffered. Having drained the royal treasury to pay his mercenary troops, Dathopa-tissa resorted to looting temples and monasteries to finance his campaign. His Tamil mercenaries also stole and shattered innumerable golden images and other objects, stole the crowning ornament of the Thuparama (which

A female deity (Tara) seated in lalitāsana pose. She wears a high beehive hair style and a band of cloth from shoulder to waist; the lower body draped. Cast in a copper alloy and gilded. 7-8th Century.

was studded with precious gems), and burned down the royal palace and the Temple of the Tooth. Their pillage was extensive. Aggabodhi's troops, led by his brother and heir apparent Kasyapa, also looted and pillaged the temples and monasteries, with Aggabodhi powerless to stop them. Finally, the tide turned against Aggabodhi, and he fled to Ruhunu, where he took ill and died.

Note: The reigns of Aggabodhi III, Dathopa-tissa I and Kasyapa II overlapped each other depending on who had the upper hand in the contest for the throne. Many writers take their reigns sequentially rather than contiguously, thus distorting the chronology of kings by about twelve years.

Kasyapa II (AD 641–650), the younger brother of Aggabodhi III, took up the fight after his older brother's death and sent Dathopa-tissa packing once more to India. His coronation did not take place immediately because of the continued unrest in the land and also because the royal paraphernalia of office had been lost. He was consecrated without the symbolic "pearl chain of one string" which his brother Aggabodhi III might have pawned in India and the crown which Dathopa-tissa might have taken with him when he fled.

Dathopa-tissa hadn't given up yet. He returned in the eighth year of Kasyapa's reign at the head of another Tamil army, was defeated, and this time was put to death. But even then the struggle wasn't over, for Dathopa-tissa's nephew, Hatthadatha, took up the cause and fled to India. Kasyapa tried to make good the damage his troops had caused the viharas and repaired and made restitution to many of them. Most of all, he was concerned for the future, for he was ill and feared Hatthadatha would return soon. Kasyapa had many children, the eldest being a son named Manavamma, but all were too young to reign; thus, to preserve the integrity of the kingdom, he selected his sister's son, Mana, a capable young man, as his heir apparent and died soon after.

Trouble began almost immediately. There was now a very large contingent of Tamil mercenaries in the capital, brought over by successive aspirants for the throne. Unable to assimilate with the local population, they became a rabble, a fifth column within the kingdom. Acutely aware of the danger they posed to the kingdom, Mana tried to expel them, but they responded by taking over the capital and inviting Hatthadatha to return from India to govern the kingdom. Mana, unnerved by such a high-stakes game, sought the help of his more experienced father, Dappula, the ruler of Ruhunu, who was hastily installed as king.

Dappula I (AD 650–650) and Mana, hoping to assuage the seething Tamil mob, signed a sham treaty with them. Fearing an impending confrontation with Hatthadatha, Mana shifted the royal treasure to Ruhunu. His caution was soon vindicated. When Hatthadatha returned with another mercenary force, local Tamils flocked to join him, and his ranks swelled as he approached the capital. Sensing sure defeat, Mana and his father fled to Ruhunu. Dappula I had been king for just one week.

Dathopa-tissa II (AD 650–658) was the kingly name chosen by Hatthadatha. He carefully cultivated the allegiance of his newfound Tamil friends and gave them positions of high office. He was also generous toward the Mahavihara, bestowing on it many favors. But he soon fell afoul of them when he built a vihara for the monks of Abhayagiri on land belonging to the Mahavihara. The monks of the Mahavihara showed their displeasure with the monarch by turning their alms bowls upside-down when they walked past his gate, in effect excommunicating him. Moreover, Mana did not remain idle for long. He soon mounted a counteroffensive from the east and south, but he lost his life in the ensuing battle. Dappula, his father, was heartbroken and died soon after. Dathopa-tissa II was now the undisputed ruler of the much-diminished Anuradhapura Kingdom.

Aggabodhi IV (AD 658–674) succeeded his cousin Dathopa-tissa II. He further assuaged the growing Tamil population by appointing many to high positions in government. One of these was Potthakuttha, a wealthy man in his own right and a generous benefactor of the Sangha who was, in the not too distant future, to play a pivotal role as kingmaker. The sixteen years of Aggabodhi's rule were a welcome respite from chaos that had preceded his tenure. There was great sadness among the people at his passing, for he had measured up to their ideal of a Dharmaraja—a righteous king. When he died, they preserved the ashes from his funeral pyre as it was believed that the ashes of a good man possessed special curative powers.

Datta (674–676 AD) was a distant member of the royal family who lived in a town near present-day Kurunagala. On the death of Aggabodhi IV, Potthakuttha imprisoned the rightful heir, Aggabodhi's brother, Dathasiva, and installed Datta as a puppet monarch. Beneath this veneer of local control, Potthakuttha, a Tamil, now held the reins of power and had effective control of the government of the Anuradhapura Kingdom.

Hatthadatha (AD 676–676) was another sham monarch installed by Potthakuttha soon after Datta's death. He lasted only six months. By the end of his reign, the country lay in ruin.

AGE OF REVIVAL

The Anuradhapura Kingdom had now lasted nearly one thousand two hundred years and the age of revival was a welcome respite for a country torn by nearly two centuries of civil war. It was a period completely free of internal turmoil.

The first ruler of the age of revival was Manavamma, who ushered in the second golden age of the Anuradhapura Kingdom. The key reason for the prosperity, stability, and continuity of government during this period was the willingness of members this dynasty to suppress their personal ambitions and follow the strict tradition of orderly dynastic succession. Even weak and incompetent rulers were never challenged by contenders to the throne. Brother followed brother, and son followed father in undisputed succession. The dynasty that reigned during the age of revival lasted nearly three hundred years, the second-longest in the island's history.

By the beginning of the seventh century, the emergence of three militaristic kingdoms in southern India would have profound impacts on the Anuradhapura Kingdom. These were the Pallavas, Pandyas, and Cholas. The Chola state, which was to play a decisive role in the future of the Anuradhapura Kingdom, had been greatly weakened by the Pallavas and played only a peripheral role during this period. The dominant power was the Pallava Kingdom. The genealogy of the rulers of this kingdom is disputed, but they may have been of Indian-Aryan/European stock from as far away as Persia who ruled over a population of Dravidian Tamil people in South India.

Thanks to the binding friendship established between Manavamma and his descendants with the rulers of Pallava, the antagonism of the recent past between the Sinhalese and the Tamils was held in check. No aspirant to the throne dared venture to India to raise armies of rebellion, nor did any south Indian princeling, chieftain, or opportunists dare mount an attack on Lanka, for they knew all too well that they would be dealt a harsh blow from the rulers of South India and Lanka. The first six rulers of the age of revival, from Manavamma through to Aggabodhi VII, had lived in the royal court of the Pallava kings and had developed enduring bonds of friendship. While the *Culavamsa* does not explicitly say so, there is no reason to doubt that there may even have been intermarriage between the two ruling families. The Tamil populace, aware of the Lankans kings' influence in their homeland, entered a state of relative docility.

During this period of peace, no developments of any great significance took place. The people's efforts were directed almost exclusively in the restoration of damaged infrastructure and in benefactions to the Sangha. Acts of their religious piety included the reconstruction of destroyed viharas, the restoration of treasures lost in the preceding period, and in celebrating dazzling religious festivals. It is no surprise that toward the latter part of the age of revival, the rising empires the Pandyas and Cholas cast their avaricious eyes on this prosperous little island.

Towards the latter part of the ninth century, the power of the Pallavas was on the wane, being replaced by the Pandyas. These rulers did not have the same bonds of friendship with the kings of the Anuradhapura Kingdom. The Pandyas, in fact, viewed the Singhalese to their south with suspicion and as a possible second front against them. Insensitive to this new geopolitical reality, a shortsighted infraction by King Sena I of the Anuradhapura Kingdom brought a swift and unexpected response from the Pandyas who attacked the Anuradhapura Kingdom and humiliated the king. This insult was soon righted by his son, who avenged the shame and installed in Pandya a ruler of his choosing. A new relationship was established, and relative calm prevailed once more over the affairs of Lanka.

Territory of the Pallava Kingdom 7th century

MANAVAMMA (AD 676–711)
Revival of Grandeur

Manavamma was only a young boy when his father king Kasyapa II chose to overlook him, because of his tender age, and hand the kingdom to his uncle Mana. As previously described, Mana's stewardship was short-lived, as he was quickly overthrown by Dathopa-tissa II. Now it came to pass that Dathopa-tissa II got wind through his spies that Manavamma was living in obscurity in a small village in Uttaradesa—the Northern Province—and planned to assassinate him. Fearing for his life, Manavamma escaped to India and entered the service of King Narasimhavarman I (AD 630–668), a king of the Pallava dynasty, who ruled large tracts of South India. Being a member of the nobility of Lanka, Manavamma was treated with great civility by the Pallava kings and soon earned their enduring trust and friendship.

Aware that Manavamma, as the scion of a noble family of Lanka, was anxious to return home and claim his inheritance, Narasimhavarman provided his friend with a fully equipped expeditionary force to regain his kingdom. Manavamma immediately set sail for Lanka, where his army soon conquered all before it. Manavamma entered Anuradhapura but did not remain there, nor waste time consecrating himself as king. Instead, he immediately set out in hot pursuit of Dathopa-tissa II, who had fled inland. Then misfortune struck Manavamma. On hearing that their king, Narasimhavarman, was gravely ill, the expeditionary army turned and returned home. Manavamma had a stalk choice: remain and face certain defeat or return to India and to fight another day. He chose to return to India, where he continued to serve his patron assiduously.

Manavamma and Narasimhavarman's grandson, later king Parameswaravarman I (AD 670–695), were of a similar age, developed a deep friendship. They fought gallantly alongside each other in the battle of Puruvalanallur in AD 674 and dealt a crushing blow to the forces of the Chalukyas who had for many years been encroaching on Pallavan territory.

Nearly twenty years had passed since Manavamma's first foray to Lanka, when the *Culavamsa* tells us, "Now the king [Parameswaravarman] thought thus: my friend serves me for the sake of the royal dignity and will become old and grey-headed thereby." Parameswaravarman graciously provided Manavamma with a new army. These troops, however, refused to cross the sea in service of any person than their monarch. According to the *Culavamsa*, Parameswaravarman withdrew with Manavamma and secretly

outfitted Manavamma in his royal amour and accouterments and then had him smuggled aboard the lead expeditionary vessel. The deception worked; the troops, thinking the king had already embarked, joined the flotilla for the journey to Lanka. [The *Culavamsa* incorrectly refers to king Narasiha, but since Manavamma probably embarked for Lanka just prior to AD 688, it was Parameswaravarman I (AD 670–695), the grandson of Narasimhavarman I, who actually assisted Manavamma.]

Manavamma's expeditionary force quickly conquered Uttaradesa. On hearing of this, Potthakuttha, who ruled the country through the puppet king Hatthadatha, immediately mounted a vigorous counterattack but his army, consisting of both Sinhalese regulars and Tamil mercenaries, was quickly defeated by Manavamma's seasoned troops.

When the people saw Hatthadatha, the hapless puppet king, fleeing the battlefield, they pounced on him and beheaded him. Potthakuttha too fled and sought refuge with a friend, a local chief. The chief, torn between his loyalty to his friend and to his king, resolved his dilemma by taking his own life rather than betray either. Potthakuttha followed the example of his friend and committed suicide too. Manavamma, by now well into middle age, entered Anuradhapura triumphantly.

While the expeditionary army probably returned home to India, it is not certain if Manavamma deported any local Tamil inhabitants too. What we do know is that Tamil domination over the affairs of state, which had been so prevalent during the reign of the three preceding kings, came to an abrupt end. He removed Tamil army commanders and courtiers from positions of authority and introduced strict controls on their activities. The local Tamil population too slipped into a period of docility which was to last for over 150 years, fully cognizant of the fact that powerful Pallavan rulers in South India would have no sympathy with them causing mischief in Lanka.

Having restored the dynasty of Silameghavanna, Manavamma set about the daunting task of the reconstruction and restitution of a kingdom devastated by over seventy years

Bodhisattva Tara stands with her right hand in a gesture of giving. In her left hand she might once have held a lotus. This 8th century, life-size, solid-cast, gilded bronze statue once had crystal and semiprecious stone inlaid eyes. The niche in the center of the headdress housed a miniature figure of a Buddha. Given its size, high quality and gilding it would have once been a prized religious object. Excavated near the east coast of Sri Lanka, it was gifted to the British Museum in 1830 by the former British Governor of Ceylon (Sri Lanka) Sir Robert Brownrigg. Thought to be too provocative, the statue was not exhibited by the museum for over thirty years.

of civil war. His descendants would rule a reenergized Anuradhapura Kingdom for the next three centuries.

Sena I (AD 831–851)
A Foolish Foreign Folly

Sena I was apprehensive about his right to the throne, because his uncle, Mahinda, the rightful heir, was still alive in exile in South India. In order to consolidate his position, Sena had Mahinda assassinated. Unfortunately, this had unforeseen consequences for the country. Sena, it appears, was totally oblivious to the titanic power struggle taking place in South India between the resurgent Pandyan Kingdom led by king Srimara Srivallabha (AD 815–62) and a weakening Pallava Dynasty who had, in the past, been the allies of the kings of Lanka. Mahinda had been living in exile under the protection of Srimara Srivallabha. In retribution for Sena's reprehensible act, Srimara Srivallabha invaded the island. He landed a large expeditionary force and took possession of the northern territory of Uttaradesa. Sena dispatched an army to expel the invaders. While Srivallabha himself led his army into battle, the Singhalese army, as a result of discordance between its generals and the king's brothers, was essentially leaderless. With a surge of support from the local Tamil population who went over to the side of the Pandya king, Sena's forces were roundly defeated.

Of the king's brothers, Kasyapa fled toward the capital, and Mahinda having witnessed the annihilation of his troops committed suicide. Sena having heard of the debacle, gathered up the royal treasure, and fled to the safety of the mountains of Malaya. Kasyapa made a last stand at the northern gates of the capital but being defeated there he fled, fought another battle at Polonnaruwa, and was captured and executed. A small garrison protecting the city immediately fled in terror, leaving the city and its great viharas and palaces brimming with treasure open to plunder. In the words of the ancient chronicle:

> "All these he took and made the Island of Lanka deprived of her valuables, leaving the splendid town in a state as if it had been plundered by Devils."

Srimara, however, had no interest in permanent conquest. Having meted out his revenge, he was now only interested in more loot. So he offered Sena a deal; he would withdraw if Sena handed over the royal treasure. Sena gladly agreed. A deal was struck, and on the very day the treasure was handed over Srimara withdrew his army and returned home.

A sullen Sena returned to the capital and set about rebuilding the devastated country and restoring peace, and to his dying day he chafed at the humiliation inflicted on him by the Pandyas.

SENA II (AD 851–885)
First Monarch to Avenge Invasions from India

Many members of the royal family and potential heirs to the throne, including Mahinda and Kasyapa, perished in the struggle against the Pandyan invasion. The kingship, therefore, passed to Sena, the son of Kasyapa, who had fought gallantly and died many years earlier.

Sena II is best remembered for avenging the humiliation and destruction inflicted on the kingdom by the marauding army of the Pandyas. Having witnessed the death of his father and uncles, the wholesale plundering of the kingdom, and the humiliation of his uncle, he was keen for the chance for vengeance. His opportunity came when Prince Varagunavarman, the son of Srimara, fell out with his father and sought Sena's help, possibly with the promise to return the royal treasure stolen by his father.

Employing his dynastic links with the Pallavan king Nandivarman III (AD 846–869), who was growing tiresome of Srimara's encroachment of his territory, Sena formed an alliance with the Pallavans and agreed to attack Srimara simultaneously. The Pallavans attacked first, and Srimara hurried north to engage them, but his army was severely defeated at the battle of Arichit in AD 860. The Sinhalese army led by an extremely capable general, the *senapati* Kutthaka, then set out for India and quickly laid waste to much of the Pandyan countryside and captured their capital of Madurai. Srimara, on hearing this, hastened back from the north, but his depleted army was no match for the Sinhalese. In the ensuing battle, Srimara was injured and perished. The victorious Sinhalese ransacked the city and, not only recovered the royal treasure the Pandyas had stolen from them, but also acquired a large quantity of Pandyan booty as well. Installing Srimara's son, Varagunavarman II (AD 862–880) as ruler of the Pandyas, the Sinhalese army returned home triumphantly. Wary of future incursions from India, Sena II set up garrisons along the coast to thwart any would-be invaders. The land was again at peace, and Sena II continued the reconstruction of the country and restoration of the capital to its former glory. He also strived to make good the losses suffered by the viharas by returning stolen treasure and replacing many lost objects.

The lesson of this intervention was not lost on the local Tamil population, for they were well aware of the wholesale destruction inflicted on the

Coming of the Sinhala, a mural at Ajanta in Cave 17.

Pandyas by a resurgent Sinhalese army. Fearing their own annihilation, they returned once more to a period of docility. These events also ensured the nonbelligerence of the Pandyas for many years to come and heralded a long period of peace.

KASYAPA V (AD 913–923)
Another Foreign Misadventure

Kasyapa V was nearly sixty years old when he became king. It was during his reign that a sequence of events took place in India that would have catastrophic long term consequences for the Anuradhapura Kingdom. The Pandyan kings in South India had been close allies of the kings of Anuradhapura since Sena II invaded the kingdom in AD 861 and installed Varagunavarman II as its ruler. Since this time, as a quid pro quo, the Pandyas discouraged any Tamil incursions into Lanka or the fomenting of unrest among the Tamil population in Lanka. Around AD 880, with the rising power of the Cholas, the geopolitical status quo in India changed drastically for the Pallava and Pandyan kingdoms. In AD 887, the Cholas lead by Aditya I annexed the remnants of the Pallava Kingdom and then turned their attention on the Pandyan Kingdom close at hand. In the ensuing years, they steadily seized the territories of the Pandyans and in AD 910, under their leader Parantaka Chola I, they attacked in force. Facing certain defeat, the Pandyan king Maravarman Rajasimha II appealed to Kasyapa V for his support against the Cholas.

Frightened by the prospect of a Chola hegemony over South India and seeing the benefit of retaining Pandya as a buffer between the expanding Chola Empire and Lanka, the king equipped an expeditionary force, appointed a competent general named Sakka*senapati* and dispatched his forces to assist the Pandyans. When Maravarman Rajasimha II saw the Sinhalese troops come ashore, he exulted, "I will join all Jambudipa [India] under one umbrella." But, at the battle of Vellur near Madurai in AD 915, even their combined might was insufficient to hold back the onslaught of the Cholas, and Maravarman Rajasimha II gave up and retreated. The valiant *senapati* Sakka and his Sinhalese troops kept up their fight, but *senapati* Sakka was soon taken ill with the plague and died. When Kasyapa V heard that his troops were perishing of the same disease, out of pity for his army, he brought them home. While the Sinhalese chronicle did not see this as a defeat, as the king withdrew his army due to illness, Parantaka Chola I, in an inscription dated AD 921, boasts of having defeated the Pandyan king Rajasimha and of having routed the army of the king of Lanka. It seems that both accounts might be correct: the Sinhalese withdrew, and the Cholas won the battle.

The Sinhalese had thrown their lot in with the Pandyans against the Cholas. This was neither forgotten nor forgiven by the Cholas. From this time onward, the fate of this little island was inextricably linked to events in India.

Dappula IV (AD 923–934)
An Unwelcome Royal Exile

Dappula IV was a younger son of Sena II. No local events of any significance are recorded during his reign. However, events in India were rapidly spinning out of control for the Pandyas in South India.

Having lost ground to the Cholas over the years, the Pandyan king Maravarman Rajasimha II, finally abandoned his kingdom and fled to Lanka, carrying with him the crown jewels and royal regalia. Dappula IV greeted the deposed king graciously, provided him with a royal stipend, and granted him a dwelling outside the city. Dappula was keen to mount an offensive against the Cholas, but clearer heads prevailed, and the king was dissuaded from such a dangerous adventure. Dappula's ministers also cautioned the king that the continued presence of Rajasimha in his kingdom presented an unacceptable risk to the nation and that he should be encouraged to leave. Rajasimha, realizing that he would not receive any further assistance from the Sinhalese, entrusted the Pandyan royal regalia with Dappula, and relocated to the home of his mother in Kerala, despite the fact that the ruler of Kerala was allied with the Cholas. There is no record of his fate thereafter.

While the military alliance between the two kingdoms was no longer in force, the kings of Anuradhapura still continued to covertly support the Pandyas against the Cholas. The Cholas, in turn, viewed the Anuradhapura Kingdom as a threat to their southern flank, a refuge for defeated Pandyan rulers, and a base for potential invasions of their territory. Added to this was the question of the Pandyan royal regalia left in the custody of the Lanka kings and the prospect of loot and the resources of this

Asvin carries a sword and circular shield, and has chains and amulets around his body, perhaps as protection. The horse too has some protection.

little island, which included pearls and gems of unsurpassed quality.

UDAYA IV (AD 945–953)
Invasion and Counter-Invasion

The *Culavamsa* describes Udaya IV as a slothful character fond of drink and with little concern for the good governance of the kingdom.

Parantaka Chola I, since his last encounter with the Sinhalese at the battle of Vellur in AD 915, on the other hand, had been preoccupied with consolidating his hold on the Pandya Empire. Having finally crushed them, he was intent on further humiliating his new subjects by having a formal coronation ceremony in their capital using the royal regalia of the Pandyan kings. As these were now in safekeeping with the Lankan king, he sent messengers to Udaya IV demanding their return. Udaya refused. Parantaka Chola I, hearing of Udaya's temperament and expecting little resistance, launched a large-scale invasion of the island to retrieve the royal regalia by force. Udaya, not expecting such a forceful response, was caught completely off guard, as his *senapati* and army were in the provinces quelling a local uprising. Hastily recalling his troops, the king marched them off to halt the invasion. Unfortunately, the *senapati* was killed in the fight, and the battle was lost. Taking the royal regalia, Udaya fled to Ruhunu, with Parantaka's forces in hot pursuit. The *Culavamsa* narrates, "The Chola troops marched thither, but finding no way of entering Ruhunu, they turned and betook themselves through fear to their own country." The *Culavamsa* account is simplistic but true, for the Chola army had won a

This statue of the hermaphrodite deity Ardhanarisvara. Divided down the middle, male on the left and female on the right it represents the unity of the male and female in the cosmos. It is unique for being the only Ardhanarisvara statue in the world in a dancing position and with the male and female sides reversed. Now at the Colombo Museum (circa 8-9th century).

Territory of the Pandya Kingdom 9th century

resounding victory, probably even entering and plundering the city of Anuradhapura. However, it did not succeed in its mission of recovering the Pandyan regalia. The reason for this was not for fear of entering Ruhunu as the *Culavamsa* would make us believe, but rather the Chola retreat was a consequence of far more pressing events taking place in India.

Parantaka Chola I, back in India, was having increasing difficulty defending his far-flung empire. In a crucial battle in AD 949, the army of Keshtrakuta Krishna III invaded the Chola Empire from the northwest, and in the ensuing battle, Parantaka's son was fatally wounded by a well-aimed arrow and his army annihilated. Confronted with this appalling setback, Parantaka Chola I could no longer pursue his venture in Lanka and withdrew his troops. The *Culavamsa* recounts the retribution meted out to Parantaka Chola I by the reenergized Sinhalese: "[They] laid waste the border-land of the Chola King and forced him with threats to restore all that he had carried away from here [as booty]." There is some uncertainty as to the meaning of this passage. Some have suggested that the Sinhalese evicted the remaining Chola troops from their island. A more likely scenario is that the Sinhalese mounted a counter-invasion, opening a second front, which helped Pandyans regain their independence from the Cholas. The Chola empire soon crumbled, and the Sinhalese recovered the booty taken away by Parantaka Chola I.

Relative peace was restored in South India, and the threat of invasion diminished for the Anuradhapura Kingdom. Albeit, this was for the shortest of time.

AGE OF COLLAPSE

The Anuradhapura Kingdom had now lasted nearly one thousand five hundred years. Conventional wisdom attributes the collapse of the Anuradhapura Kingdom to the invasion of the island by the army of the Chola emperor Rajaraja in AD 993. This view is overly simplistic and ignores more serious maladies that plagued the kingdom for some time.

In the preceding Age of Revival, inspirational leaders such as Manavamma and his descendants had reenergized the nation after an earlier period of civil war and anarchy. The kingdom's vast irrigation infrastructure was repaired, and the economy revived. Religious establishments too were restored, although not to the same grandeur of the past. Importantly the normally passive Singhalese people took up arms and not only thwarted several invasions from India but actively took the fight back the continent and demonstrated that they were a force to be reckoned with. While the nation was now more militaristic, it was also more fractious, less religious, and less virile than it had been at its zenith. As time passed a confluence of events hastened the rapid collapse of the Anuradhapura Kingdom.

The seeds of destruction were sown when an aging king, who ruled a strong and prosperous kingdom, took a young Kalinga princess as his queen. On his death, this queen and her cohorts vested control of the government, and within just ten years, ran the country to ground. Unpopular with the local citizenry, they imported large numbers of foreign mercenaries and administrators to govern the kingdom and then failed to exercise effective control over them. These administrators, unfamiliar with the levers of government and more interested in lining their own pockets, mismanaged the economy and the kingdom's vast irrigation systems, leading to a drastic drop in food production, economic activity, and subsequently in tax revenues. The mercenaries too, left unsupervised, soon commenced an orgy of looting, extortion, and standover tactics with the population. Rising lawlessness led to the abandonment of the capital by the local aristocracy, administrators, and merchants. The situation rapidly spiraled out of control. The young and inexperienced prince who eventually inherited the kingdom tried heroically to remedy the situation, but it was too late. Finally, in despair, he abandoned his kingdom to the rabble.

Rajaraja, the Chola emperor, seeing an opportunity too good to miss invaded the island and snuffed out the Anuradhapura Kingdom

MAHINDA IV (AD 956–972)
Dangerous Dalliances in Love and War

Mahinda IV was most likely the son of Kasyapa V. On his accession, he acted quickly to quash an uprising against him and succeeded in establishing hegemony over the entire island, including the always intransigent princedom of Ruhunu.

Mahinda had a queen named Kitti, but the *Culavamsa* states that: "although there was also in Lanka a race of nobles, the Ruler of men had a princess of the line of the Ruler of Kalinga fetched and made her his mahesi [queen]." The reason for this union can only be described as an act of pure vanity on the part of an old man. While the connections between the aristocratic families of Lanka and those of Kalinga go all the way back to Vijaya, this was clearly a marriage of desire rather than a geopolitical alliance. This foolish dalliance with the Kalinga princess would have catastrophic consequences for the kingdom.

In about the eighth year of his reign, Mahinda was confronted with an incursion by a foreign ruler, the *Culavamsa* refers to as the "Vallabha king." Mahinda dispatched an army commanded by his *senapati* named Sena to meet this threat. The invaders were stymied, a treaty signed, and the foreigners expelled. The leader referred to as Vallabha was probably Parantaka Chola II, also known as Sundara Chola, the grandson of Parantaka Chola I and the ruler of a newly resurgent Chola Kingdom (the term Vallabha probably refers to the Tamil word "Valavan" and is used by the *Culavamsa* as an epithet for Chola.) The Cholas gained no advantage from this invasion other than possibly an undertaking from Mahinda to refrain from supporting the Pandyans.

An inscription by Mahinda IV at Vessagiriya reads in part, "who [Mahinda] has brought to his feet all the riches of the whole of Dambadiva [India] by means of the valor of his commander in chief Sena." This overt declaration is a potent harbinger of things to come, as it appears that *senapati* Sena had become a powerful figure in the king's court.

The *Culavamsa* records Mahinda's many acts of munificence, his concern for the well-being of the Sangha, and his promulgation of rules for the proper administration of important establishments in the capital. He also repaired many dilapidated reservoirs to put an end to recurring food scarcity. Judging by his record, he ruled over a vibrant kingdom.

The central figure is that of Bodhisattva Avalokitesvara (the bodhisattva of compassion) with a carving of the meditating Buddha in its headdress. The female figure to the left is thought to be his consort Tara and the figure on the right their son Prince Sudhana. 10th century Mahayana Buddhist low-relief rock carving with part of the original plaster and paint intact. Buduruwagala

Sena V (AD 972–981)
A Hapless Boy King and the Destruction of a Kingdom

Sena V was only twelve years old when he ascended the throne on the death of his father, Mahinda IV. His elevation to the position of king at such a young age suggests that the queen mother, the Kalinga queen, with the help of the ex-king's chief of the army, *senapati* Sena, engineered the young boy's accession. The young king retained Sena as his *senapati*, but they soon fell out over an indiscretion by the queen mother. *Senapati* Sena had a younger brother name Mahamalla, who the king discovered was sleeping with his mother, the queen, so he had the man executed. The king then appointed a trusted court official named Udaya as his new *senapati*. *Senapati* Sena, who was away in an outlying province at the time, was furious and marched immediately to the capital. Terrified, the boy king fled with his entourage to the safety of Ruhunu. The queen mother, no doubt angry with her son for murdering her lover, escaped and returned to the capital. There she and *senapati* Sena connived to take control of the government.

Why *senapati* Sena, a celebrated war hero who did not covet the throne himself, chose to side with the Kalinga queen is uncertain. The execution of his brother for the serious crime of sleeping with the queen alone seems unlikely to have caused him to abandon his people and switch his allegiances. Was *senapati* Sena also from Kalinga with little loyalty to the kingdom? Or was he having an affair with the Kalinga queen himself? Besot by her, did he betray his king and country for the carnal pleasures of this woman? We do not know.

The local aristocracy and the Sangha did not back this power grab. The army which had, under the command of *senapati* Sena himself, been victorious against the Cholas just a few years earlier seems to have disintegrated. In order to bolster their position and marginalize those who had sided with the king, *senapati* Sena imported a large number of foreign mercenaries and administrators into the country. While the *Culavamsa* is silent on the numbers, the *Rājāvaliya* and the *Pujavali* claim, probably exaggerated, that they numbered ninety-five thousand.

The exiled king made a desperate attempt to reclaim his throne. Mustering up a militia, he marched on the capital, but *senapati* Sena and his foreign mercenaries annihilated the king's forces. Having defeated the king, *senapati* Sena had no interest in governing the country. He handed over the administration of the kingdom to these foreigners and withdrew to his residence at Polonnaruwa.

With no credible counterforce to hold them in check, these mercenaries—these foreign soldiers of fortune—now turned against their patrons. Disorganized and leaderless, their numbers quickly degenerated into unruly mobs that looted, expropriated property, ransacked viharas, and intimidated the people. No attempt, it seems, was made to control their rampage. This suggests that either the *senapati* Sena and the Kalinga queen had lost control of the situation, or a more Machiavellian reason was that the upheaval inflicted more damage on the local Singhalese fraction supporting their inefficacious king and his aristocrats, thereby strengthening the hand of the Kalinga fraction consisting of the Kalinga queen, *senapati* Sena and their foreign supporters.

Dismayed by the chaos, a deputation of citizens beseeched their exiled monarch to act. In order to save his kingdom, the king, on the advice of his ministers, opened negotiations with *senapati* Sena. It was a humiliating outcome for the young sovereign. He was forced to banish his most trusted minister Udaya and also take *senapati* Sena's daughter as his queen. He was then forced to reside in Polonnaruwa, under virtual house arrest, where a watchful eye was kept on him by the Kalinga faction. After his capitulation, the king became a mere figurehead. Despondent, he took to drink and spent his time cavorting with his "low-class favorites."

The foreign administrators installed in high positions of government by *senapati* Sena had no understanding of the management of a sophisticated hydraulic society such as that of the Anuradhapura Kingdom. Critical repairs and maintenance to vital infrastructure was neglected. Reservoirs and channels silted up or were otherwise damaged. Farmers were harassed, and their crops stolen. As a consequence, agricultural production plummeted. This, in turn, affected tax revenue. With dwindling revenue, the state was incapable of paying the wages of the foreign mercenaries and administrators, further exacerbating a dangerous situation. Political decay had by now permeated through all levels of government. Corruption, nepotism, and incompetence were rampant. As the government grew more and more oppressive, those who could abandoned the capital and escaped to the countryside. The wealthy classes in order to avoid the rising terror as well as to evade punitive taxes then set up their own independent fiefdoms.

The situation was spinning out of control. *Senapati* Sena, possibly ailing, exercised no control. The Kalinga-queen was so despised that she lacked any credible support. The young king, the scion of a great dynasty, was usually intoxicated, befuddled, and incapable of governing.

The breakdown of authority during this regime was so profound that the once magnificent city was now a war zone with armed gangs of all persuasions roaming the streets, plundering and terrorizing the citizenry with impunity. No one in power, it seemed, cared.

King Sena V died at the age of just twenty-two.

MAHINDA V (AD 986–1029)
Last King of the Anuradhapura Kingdom

Mahinda V was the younger brother of the preceding king Sena V and the son of Mahinda IV and a lesser queen. He was not an offspring of the Kalinga queen. The fact that Mahinda V, who would have been barely an adult at best, was not challenged by the Kalinga faction suggests that *senapati* Sena and the Kalinga-queen might have died before this time or that on the death of Sena V the Sinhalese fraction reasserted itself and restored a prince with "untainted" blood to the throne of Lanka. *Senapati* Sena and the Kalinga queen, who had brought such misery and wanton destruction upon the nation from which it would never recover, ignominiously disappeared from history.

Mahinda V inherited a kingdom in turmoil. The *Culavamsa* describes the ill-omened start of his reign as follows:

> The Prince Mahinda raised the white umbrella in splendid Anuradhapura which was full of strangers brought hither by the senapati Sena and abode there for ten years amid difficult circumstances.

The *Culavamsa's* assessment of the situation is indeed a gross understatement. The situation was unimaginably dire. The city was awash with the foreigners brought over by *senapati* Sena and the Kalinga queen. Their rampages had left Anuradhapura a barren and desolate place. Most of its citizens had fled. Buildings lay ruined and abandoned. Only thugs and the destitute dared wander its debris-strewn streets.

Bravely had Mahinda V returned to the capital for his consecration ceremony and took up residence there. Well-intentioned and young in years, he had arrived with determination and a heartfelt hope of restoring normalcy to his beleaguered kingdom. He strove assiduously for nearly ten years to rebuild his ravaged kingdom, but it was to no avail. It was too little, too late.

Commanding little authority and with no political and administrative experience, the task at hand was daunting for the ill-fated king. His situation was so dire, and his government so dysfunctional, that when peasants refused to pay their taxes, he was powerless to enforce his will on them as his mercenary army had not been paid and was near revolt. For a while, the hapless king contained his mutinous troops by paying their salaries from the royal purse but soon these reserves were exhausted. A mob of mercenaries the king himself had brought over from Kerala in South India were so bellicose that armed with bows and arrows, swords and other weapons, they blockaded the royal palace and yelled, "So long as there is no pay he shall not eat." Mahinda was penniless.

With its economy faltering, its cities and towns plundered, its fields and crops ravaged, its citizenry robbed and terrorized, its country-side infested by marauding bandits, the kingdom teetered on the brink of collapse.

In 992 AC, one thousand three hundred and seventy years after the founding of the city of Anuradhapura, Mahinda V, the last king of the Anuradhapura Kingdom, secretly escaped from his palace through an underground tunnel and fled the capital–abandoning his kingdom to a seething rabble.

Abandoned and ungoverned, warlords and militias divvied up the spoils among themselves. The Kingdom of Anuradhapura was now in its final death throes.

It wasn't long before Rajaraja I (AD 985–1014), the ruler of the Chola Empire of South India, got wind of Mahinda's plight and his abandonment of his kingdom.

Rajaraja was the son of Parantaka Chola II. Having recently subdued the Pallavas, Pandyan, and the Cheras, he was the supreme overload of South India. A man with a grand vision, he was now intent on dominating the lucrative east-west trade routes passing through the Indian Ocean. Possessing the little island of Lanka to his south, the entreport between east and west was an opportunity too good for him to pass up. Rajaraja also held many grudges against the people of the little island to his south. Was it not they who had sided with the Pandyans, Pallavans, and Cheras against the Cholas in wars past? Was it not this little island that had thwarted the ambitions of his father Parantaka Chola II and even refused to hand over the royal regalia of the Pandyan kings which his

Wheel thrown high fired plain red ware from the late Anuradhapura Period, with punctuated embossed decorated band around the shoulder; primarily for storing grain and goods.

grandfather, Parantaka Chola I, had waged war to regain? The time was right, no doubt, for him to pluck the ripened fruit and make Lanka his.

In AD 993 Rajaraja Chola I dispatched an invading army to Lanka. He was right; his well-disciplined troops quickly swept away the feeble resistance they encountered and lay waste both the countryside and the ragtag armies of the warlords who opposed him. The local Tamil populace and mercenaries quickly came over to his side. His men soon entered the undefended capital and commenced an orgy of looting, pillaging, and raping. Indiscriminately they murdered and stole anything they could get their hands on. Viharas and palaces, looted many times before, were plundered once more, their inhabitants tortured and murdered. Having stripped the city of all its treasure, the Cholas torched the remnants of the once magnificent city of Anuradhapura and moved their capital to Polonnaruwa. The wretched survivors watched in horror as their beloved city was destroyed.

News of the final destruction of Anuradhapura sent shockwaves across the country. Their city which had survived for over a millennium and a half. The center of their religion and culture had been obliterated. It appeared to the people as though their whole world had been consumed.

The core territory of the Anuradhapura Kingdom was quickly occupied. Renamed Mummudi-sola-mandalam, it became a mere province of the burgeoning Chola empire. Polonnaruwa, their new capital, was renamed Jananatha-mangalam after a well-known title of Rajaraja I. To commemorate his victory, Rajaraja had a stone temple to Siva constructed at Polonnaruwa. This beautiful little temple is one of the few Hindu monuments of antiquity still standing in a good state of preservation today. There are no Chola buildings or monuments in Anuradhapura.

The copper plates inscribed during the reign of his son Rajendra I (AD 1014-1044) at the Thiruvalangadu Siva temple in Trivellore, India, in verse 80 offer, with some hyperbole, a glowing account of Rajaraja's invasion of Lanka, drawing parallels between the invasions of the island by Rama of the *Ramayana* legend with the exploits of his illustrious father:

> Rama constructing a bridge across the water of the ocean with the assistance of able monkeys, killed with great difficulty the king of Lanka with sharp-edged arrows; but this terrible general of that king Arulmozhivarman [Rajaraja] crossed the ocean by ships and burnt the Lord of Lanka. Hence Rama is surely surpassed by this.

Only Ruhunu, always the bulwark and the sanctuary of the Sinhalese in times of adversity, resisted the onslaught of the Chola army and remained independent. There Mahinda V resided in doleful exile. Although the rightful king of all of Lanka, he was, in truth, now only the ruler of a tiny province in the southernmost part of the island.

Unlike previous Chola invasions, which were mostly opportunistic excursions in search of plunder, the wider aim of the Cholas this time was the maritime domination of the Indian Ocean. For this reason, the annexation of the entire island and its ports was crucial to their grand design. In about AD 1017, Rajendra Chola I, the son of Rajaraja Chola I, commenced a new campaign to conquer the whole island.

While the Cholas ruled territory to the north, Mahinda had remained in his southern sanctuary of Ruhunu as its titular ruler. In the thirty-sixth year of his reign, misfortune befell him once more. The *Culavamsa* (ch. LV, v.16-19) narrates:

> In the thirty-sixth year of the King's reign the Cholas seized the Queen, the jewels, the diadem, that he had inherited, the whole of the royal ornaments, the priceless diamond bracelet a gift of the gods, the unbreakable sword and the relic of the torn strip of cloth. But the ruler himself fled to the jungle, they captured alive with the pretense of making a treaty.

The *Karandai* plates (ll,135-39,141) of Rajendra I inscribed in AD 1017 confirm the accuracy of account given in the *Culavamsa* in two verses.

> He took with his great fierce army the crown of the war-like king if Ilam [Lanka] on the sea, the exceeding beautiful crown of the queen of that king, the beautiful crown and pearl necklace of India which the Pandyan had previously deposited with that king, and the entirety of Ila-mandalam on the heaving sea.

Mahinda had now lost all he possessed. By losing the royal regalia he had suffered the ultimate humiliation and forfeited his right to rule. The possession of the royal regalia which included the *senachatra* and the "pearl chain of one string" were symbols of royal dignity—a king's right to rule. A new king was always keen to take ownership of these to legitimize his rule. Moggallana I quickly took possession of these when Kasyapa I committed suicide. Aggabodhi III, on the other hand, fled with the "pearl chain of one string," (which he might have pawned and is probably the same chain subsequently referred to as the pearl necklace of India in the Karandai plates of Rajendra I) as proof of his royal identity. Consequently, his successor, Dathopa-tissa I, who did not have the chain for his coronation, was thought to have his royal dignity wanting. Similarly, when the umbrella of Sangha-tissa II accidentally fell into the hands of the rebel Moggallana III the army at once recognized Moggallana as the legitimate king. Only once before had these fallen into foreign hands, having always been spirited away to safety in times of danger. The Chola king's custody of these symbols of kingship conferred on him symbolic dominion over the Anuradhapura Kingdom.

Rajendra's troops plundered and looted an already improvised kingdom, even breaking open holy relic chambers and stealing their precious contents. Then they ransacked Ruhunu, which had withstood all previous attempts to plunder it. Carts loaded with treasure trundled toward the ports, soldiers weighed down with booty staggered northward. The rape of Lanka was complete.

There are conflicting views of the extent of the Chola hegemony over Lanka. It appears that Raja Rata, the core territory of the Anuradhapura Kingdom, acquiesced to Chola rule without a fight while Ruhunu, although subjugated, always retained its defiance to Chola rule and in time the Sinhala nation would rise again like a phoenix from this province.

Territory of the Chola Kingdom, 11th century

Mahinda V, his queen, and the royal regalia were shipped back to India. There the last king of the Anuradhapura Kingdom, a man who had tried heroically to revive his kingdom and failed, died in captivity in 1029.

The *Culavamsa* describes Mahinda V, the last king of Anuradhapura, as of very weak character. This might indeed have been true. But his was a herculean task, and he was only human—young, inexperienced, and alone. Failure was inevitable.

Ruins of the Abhayagiri as seen by Jonathan Forbes in 1828.

ABANDONMENT

The abandonment of the city of Anuradhapura did not bring about its immediate disappearance from the public psyche. With the neglect of the great irrigation works on which this civilization thrived, the productivity of the land plummeted. Clogged canals and reservoirs became breeding grounds for mosquitoes. Malaria, famine, and neglect sapped the virility of the populace. The survivors slowly drifted away.

The city continued to be of religious significance for at least another two hundred years, but slowly this once grand metropolis with its great monasteries fell into eerie silence, occasionally disturbed by the slither of a snake or the chirping of a lonesome bird or two. Its magnificent monasteries overgrown with vegetation, their walls and roofs pierced and disemboweled by the ceaseless thrust of trees and tangled roots slowly crumbled. The gleaming white dagobas that had once soared so majestically into the skyline became huge, tree-covered hillocks the size of small towns. These monoliths loomed forlorn, over the surrounding landscape. Over the ensuing centuries, a handful of its most sacred shrines continued to be tended to by a few devote and intrepid monks who braved the hostile environment around them and eked out a meager existence among its ruins. The faint glimmer of their lamplight flickered through the night, revealing the colossi of a once mighty city.

A number of latter-day kings attempted to restore some of its great monuments. The decay, however, was too great for their resources to reverse.

By the census of 1871, the population density of the area had declined from as many as two thousand five hundred persons per square mile to only sixteen persons per square mile. The population of Buddhist monks had declined from more than twenty-five thousand in Anuradhapura alone to a mere two thousand four hundred throughout the entire island.

For nearly one thousand four hundred years, Anuradhapura flourished to become one of the great kingdoms of the ancient world, then only to be snuffed out, abandoned, engulfed by forest, and forgotten.

For centuries it lay hidden, lost in the jungle, relegated to the realms of dimming folk memory.

*Ruins of the Abhayagiri Vihara
(photograph dated 1885)*

REDISCOVERY

Robert Knox, an Englishman who escaped from nineteen years of captivity in the Kandyan Kingdom in Malaya country in central Sri Lanka, made his escape through Anuradhapura in 1679. He described the ruins of this once magnificent city and the watch kept by devoted Buddhist monks:

> Near by is a River, by which we came when we made our escape: all along which is abundance of hewed stones, some long for Pillars, some broad for paving. Over this River there have been three Stone Bridges built upon Stone Pillars, but now are fallen down; and the Countrey all desolate without Inhabitants. At this City of Anurodgburro is a Watch kept.

In 1820 Ralph Backhaus, a young British civil servant, is credited with being the first Westerner in modern time to "discover" Anuradhapura. He reported a great ruined city hidden in massive tropical forest, with malaria-infested reservoirs and a few isolated, ill-nourished, disease-ridden people around its ruins. Robert Davey, in his book *An Account of the Interior of Ceylon and of its inhabitants* published in 1821, wrote as follows:

> Anooradapoora, so long the capital of Ceylon, is now a small mean village, in the mists of a desert. A larger tank, numerous stone pillars, two or three immense tumuli (probably old dagobahs,) are the principal remains. It is still considered a sacred spot; and is a place of pilgrimage.

In that same year, Lieutenant Mitchell Henry Fagan of the Second Ceylon Regiment, also forcing his way through almost impenetrable forest, reported how he came face to face with a colossal statue gazing out at him from the foliage. Major Jonathan Forbes, who in 1831 would be the first Westerner to "discover" Sigiriya, visited Anuradhapura in 1828, noting that "the only place clear of jungle was in front of the Maha-vihara [great temple], where a shady tree occupies the center of the square." The Thuparama was a jumble of pillars and stones, and the other great dagobas were little more than steep-sided mounds covered with thick forest

The rediscovery of Anuradhapura stimulated keen interest in the Western world and dispelled the notion that the locals were uncivilized savages.

After nearly a thousand years of oblivion, the grand city is finally being excavated and conservation work has led to the rediscovery of an exquisite royal city of temples and monasteries.

PART 2 - THE KINGDOM

This carving depicts a king with his parasol-bearer and a young attendant mounted on an elephant in a procession. It is probably similar to that of many centuries earlier. This chest was made of ivory, gold, rubies and sapphires in Sri Lanka around 1543.

GOVERNMENT

Four dynasties ruled during the nearly one thousand five hundred years of the Anuradhapura Kingdom. These were the Vijayan (483 BC–AD 127), First Lambakanna (AD 127–433), Moriya (AD 460–693), and Second Lambakanna (AD 693–1012) dynasties. There were also a number of interdynastic periods during which the country was governed by both local and foreign interlopers. Kings were expected to be of the Kshatriya caste, and kingship usually passed to the oldest surviving male member of the royal family. In many instances, this meant that the king's brother, who may have been well advanced in years, rather than his oldest son inherited the throne. In the absence of a suitable candidate, matrilineal descent was also sometimes accepted. Kings married within the royal family and sometimes into the ruling houses of foreign kingdoms, particularly the Kalinga Kingdom of India (thus maintaining a link to the original Vijayan lineage.) A new monarch was legitimized through a consecration ceremony referred to as the *abhiseka*. The main symbol of royal dignity was the *senachatra*—"a white parasol" and the *ekavali*—"pearl chain of one string."

A loose feudal system of government based on customs, traditions, and the Buddhist dharma were used as the basis of law. This system of government lacked the rigid authoritarianism usually associated with feudal societies elsewhere. The monarch held absolute power but was nevertheless expected to conform to the rules of the Buddhist dharma, the universal laws governing human existence and conduct. He was expected to rule as a Dharmaraja, "a just king." He was not to indulge in self-aggrandizement, so with the exception of Kasyapa I, we see no grandiose royal palaces or mausoleums.

The king's kinsman held most high offices. The day-to-day affairs of each village, however, were managed by a local committee composed of village elders. The king was the final arbiter in all legal disputes and was the promulgator of all laws. The chief judicial officer was known as *viniccayamacca,* under whom were a number of lesser officials known as *vinicchayaka*. Village headmen and provincial governors adjudicated in local matters. In general, justice was administered leniently. However, crimes such as treason, murder, and slaughter of cattle were generally punishable by death.

RELIGION

The history of Anuradhapura was inextricably linked with the establishment and consolidation of Buddhism in Sri Lanka. From the outset, it had a profound impact on the people's psyche and spurred them to great feats of engineering, arts, and culture.

The impact of Buddhism in molding the character of Sinhalese civilization can be summarized by three pivotal events. The first was the conversion of King Devanampiya-tissa to Buddhism in 249 BC. With royal patronage Buddhism quickly permeated through all levels of society, binding the people with a common religion, language, and script. This, in turn, expedited the political and cultural unification of the country. Buddhism quickly eclipsed Brahmanism, Jainism, and other religions to become the preeminent religion of the Sinhalese nation. Imbued by their new religion, the first significant edifices such as the Thuparama and Isurumuniya were built. The second was the planting of the sapling of the Bodhi Tree under which Buddha is said to have gained enlightenment. The planting of this sapling in a park especially set aside by King Devanampiya-tissa lay the foundations for the Mahavihara (Great Monastery), for many years, the central religious orthodox on the island. This further galvanized the nation and set it apart from its neighbor to the north. The third was the arrival in AD 371 of the Tooth Relic, believed to be the left canine tooth of Buddha. This cemented the country's role as the last bastion of Buddhism, which by this time was fast disappearing from India. The Tooth Relic soon became the central focus of religious veneration.

Buddhism itself was transformed by the assimilation of the beliefs and exorcistic ceremonies of existing local cults. Its precept of tolerance meant that the people had a large degree of acceptance of other religions. Over time, isolated from the religious upheavals in India, Buddhism flourished in the insularity of this island.

The first great religious fraternity was the Mahavihara or "Great Monastery," established by King Devanampiya-tissa in 249 BC. For the next two hundred eighteen years, it reigned supreme as the custodian of Buddhism on the island.

Samadhi Buddha
5th century

In 31 BC the Abhayagiri monastery complex was constructed by King Vattagamani-abhaya (29–17 BC). Flouting custom, he bequeathed his new monastery to Mahā-Tissa, a monk who had supported him during his many years in exile. Initially, this vihara was also affiliated with the Mahavihara. Shortly afterward, however, the monks of the Mahavihara, either out of self-interest or pique at the king's favoritism toward his new vihara, expelled Mahā-Tissa from the Mahavihara "for frequenting the families of laymen." The Mahavihara's high-handedness led to a mass exodus of monks from the elitist and sumptuous lifestyle of the Mahavihara to the more austere existence practiced at Abhayagiri. No longer constrained by the stifling orthodoxy of the Mahavihara, in about 17 BC, the Abhayagiri monks adopted the more enlightened approach to religion being advocated by an Indian monk named Dhammaruci forming the Abhayagiri fraternity. For the next two centuries the two fraternities coexisted, both following a common doctrine and supported equally by the monarchs of the day.

The accession of King Mahasena to the throne in AD 334 all but destroyed the Mahavihara. Urged on by a monk named Samghhamitta who had tutored him as a child, the king outlawed the Mahavihara, reducing its monks to destitution and forcing them to abandon their monasteries. The Abhayagiri vihara benefited handsomely from the misfortunes of the Mahavihara and increased its power to the point that even the king was wary of confronting it. Over a period that lasted nearly seven hundred years it eclipsed the Mahavihara and became the preeminent religious establishment of the land. Unable to bring the powerful Abhayagiri to heel, and still dissatisfied with the much weakened Mahavihara, Mahasena set about upstaging them both by creating a brand-new monastery. Appropriating a large tract of land belonging to the Mahavihara known as the Jotivana Gardens, the king constructed the largest dagoba ever built, intent on dwarfing all the dagobas of the Mahavihara and Abhayagiri. He then installed a group of dissatisfied monks from Abhayagiri, known as the Sagalikas, at his new monastery. They came to be known as the Jetavana fraternity.

Of the three fraternities, the Mahavihara adhered strictly to the Theravada doctrine; the monks of Abhayagiri, at various times, followed Theravada, Mahayana and Vajrayana doctrines and the Jetavana fraternity followed a variation of Theravada. In their heyday, there were seventeen monastic complexes belonging to the fraternities located in the city alone. These monasteries collectively had in excess of twenty thousand monks.

Inspired by their religion and anxious to gain merit, king and commoner alike vied with one another in their magnanimous support of these monasteries, building grandiose dagobas and making generous donations to these establishments and to their burgeoning population of clergy. Monasteries thus acquired large tracts of prime land. Some of this land the monks farmed themselves, some they gave away to curry favor with high officials and the rest they rented out to tenant farmers in return for a share of the crop. These harvests, together with donations from pious devotees, gave these monks tremendous economic leverage. As these monasteries expanded over the centuries, they resembled miniature cities. In addition to the monks and novices the monasteries also employed administrators, singers, drummers, dancers, tenant farmers, and slaves. They also helped the needy such as widows and orphans.

Over time the power and wealth of these institutions grew so immense that their influence extended well beyond religion and into the realm of secular politics. In time large portions of the country's wealth were diverted for the maintenance of these enormous religious establishments, which drained the treasury and, at times, nearly bankrupted the country. By the time of the demise of the Anuradhapura Kingdom in the tenth century, these monasteries while still vital to the economy because of their vast holdings of productive land, had fallen in to disrepute and had dwindled to a mere fraction of their former prestige, having little impact on the affairs of the people and government.

A 20th century image of a farmer plowing a field, probably unchanged from ancient times.

ECONOMY

The economy of the Anuradhapura Kingdom was primarily agrarian. An extensive system of interconnected irrigation works consisting of vast water reservoirs (referred to locally as tanks), canals, and channels enabled large tracks of semiarid land to be brought under cultivation. These irrigation systems were the lifeblood of this hydraulic society, and as such, it was seen as the primary responsibility of the sovereign to ensure their upkeep.

Rice, the principal crop, was grown in abundance. Cotton and sugarcane were also cultivated in significant quantities. Oxen and buffalo were used as draft animals for plowing, threshing, and cartage. In this Buddhist country, the slaughter of animals was considered unclean. Animal husbandry was limited to raising cattle for milk, curd, buttermilk, ghee, and butter. The numerous tanks provided an ample supply of freshwater fish. Saltwater fishing was not widely practiced, for most of the populace lived a fair distance from the coast.

A network of roads, both paved and unpaved, wide enough to accommodate a bullock-drawn cart, were built. Chariots, too, were in use, but primarily as an instrument of war. Elephants were the heavy lifters and movers of the day. The bridges, which were mostly made of wood, have long since perished. Some, such as the Gal Palama near Anuradhapura, were sturdy structures capable of supporting the weight of fully laden elephants.

The country had its own supply of important metals, such as iron, copper, silver, and gold. Metallurgy was quite advanced, featuring the large-scale production of iron and steel implements and weapons. Surpluses in agriculture and the general prosperity of the populace supported a large population of officials, monks, artisans, and scholars.

During the dry season, villagers engaged in slash-and-burn agriculture. Small plots of forest were cleared to grow crops such as ginger, melon, and vegetables. To protect their little plots, known as chenas, from marauding wild animals, especially elephants, the villagers built small huts atop sturdy trees. From these perches, the cultivators beat drums and made other loud noises to scare wild animals away from their precious crops.

Revenue was raised by taxation, including land tax, a water tax, import and export duties, fines (a fine for adultery is recorded), and licenses. The primary tax was the *bojakapati* (grain tax), which was one-sixth of the income derived from an agricultural property. A *dakapati* (water tax) was levied on water used from reservoirs. Customs duties were also imposed on imports and exports (a reference to the tax on the export of elephants is recorded). Taxes could be paid in cash or by the provision of one's personal labor for public works projects, such as repairing roads and reservoirs. The king was also entitled to demand *rajakariya*, or compulsory labor, from all landholders to aid the major works, such as road construction and irrigation projects. The king's treasurer, the *badagarika*, was responsible for collecting taxes.

The country's strategic location at the crossroads of the East and West, its excellent natural harbors at Mahatittha and Gokanna (Mannar and Trincomalee), and the desirability of its commodities made the island an entrepôt for traders since prehistoric times.

Merchants from Persia, Ethiopia, Yemen, China, and India exchanged their commodities in Sri Lankan ports. Special areas were set aside in the cities and ports for their residences and bazaars. The kingdom's primary exports were gems, spices, pearls, elephants, ivory, and tortoise, turtle, and conch shells.

The country's key imports were silk and ceramics from China; perfumes, wines, glass, and horses from Persia and Egypt; textiles, silver, iron cauldrons, camphor, sandalwood, basalt, marble, and copper from India; and lapis lazuli from Afghanistan. Horses were so highly prized that their importation was exempt from taxes.

SECURITY

Being a Buddhist land whose people abhorred violence, the kingdom, rarely maintained a large, standing army. This profound indifference to the military proved to be, time and again, the Achilles' heel of the Sinhalese people. Though frequently invaded by foreign marauders, the Sinhalese rarely mounted foreign incursions of their own, with rare exceptions during the reigns of Sena II (AD 851–885) when a large expeditionary force mounted a very successful foray against kingdoms in South India.

In times of crisis, the king had the right to demand one able-bodied son from every family in the kingdom for military service. The army consisted of the *Chaturangani Sena* (Fourfold Army), which included an elephant corps, cavalry, chariots, and infantry. The infantry consisted of swordsmen, spearmen, and archers. These troops were supplemented by foreign mercenaries. These mercenaries were usually from South India and were employed in large numbers, especially during the latter part of the Anuradhapura period. Considering that most foreign invasions of the kingdom originated in southern India, the employment of mercenaries from this area seems foolhardy.

The king usually led his troops into battle mounted on a richly adorned war elephant. The Kshatriya caste to which most kings belonged, adhered to a strict code of chivalry. It was not uncommon for kings or commanders to engage in single man-to-man combat. The outcome of the entire confrontation could be determined by this single battle, avoiding unnecessary bloodshed—for example, as in Dutugamunu's final battle with Elara.

Strangely, for an island nation subjected to frequent seaborne invasions, a regular navy was rarely maintained. This was another failing for which the country paid dearly.

ARCHITECTURE

The Anuradhapura Kingdom was located in the semiarid north-central plains of Sri Lanka. From the very outset, prodigious amounts of collective energy were expended in building and maintaining extensive systems of reservoirs to capture and store precious rainwater brought by monsoonal rains. These were interconnected with canals and channels to collect and distribute water over vast tracts of land. Any depression of significance was dammed, and its water harvested. At its zenith, the city had some of the most sophisticated irrigation systems of the ancient world. The discovery of the principle of the valve tower, or valve pit, for regulating the escape of water from a dam was invented by these people. Today, nearly two thousand years later, many of these ancient irrigation works have been recommissioned for use in modern agriculture. These are some of the oldest surviving man-made reservoirs in the world.

The key architectural achievements of the period radiated around the city of Anuradhapura. In addition to the irrigation works, huge brick dagobas were constructed to enshrine objects of veneration. The Thuparama, built by Devanampiya-tissa in the third century BC, was the first of these structures, said to enshrine collarbone of Buddha. The Ruwanwelisaya, Abhayagiri, and Jetavana dagobas were the largest brick structures ever constructed, smaller only than the largest pyramids of Egypt. Around these dagobas were huge monastic complexes that at one time accommodated as many as twenty thousand monks. These structures were adorned with elaborately carved buildings, sculptures, and carvings painted in bright colors.

Most secular buildings, including the royal palaces, were built of brick and wood. Little evidence of these structures remains today. We understand from ancient records that many of these buildings were multistoried and colorfully decorated.

The common people lived in small one- or two-roomed dwellings with thatched roofs. Kitchens and toilet facilities were outside these dwellings.

SOCIETY

The caste system in Sri Lanka, tempered by the influence of Buddhism, evolved its own distinct characteristics. Although it shared the occupational stratification of the Indian model, it had neither an exclusive Brahmanic social hierarchy nor the concept of defilement by contact with impure persons or substances. It is important to note that the concept of race and ethnicity, as we understand it today, was of little importance. Caste was the overarching social delineator, even more powerful than that of religion. King and commoner alike married within their caste. For this reason, for example, kings always married other Kshatriyas, irrespective of ethnicity.

Women appear to have enjoyed considerable freedom and independence in the context of the time. Some might have been wealthy in their own right. A number of cave inscriptions record that these dwellings were donated by women. The first female monarch, Queen Anula, ascended the throne in 47 BC, making her a compatriot of Cleopatra of Egypt. Although it is not clear whether women enjoyed true equality with men, there was no discrimination on matters of religion.

Slavery was not prevalent. Indentured servitude, usually as a consequence of poverty or debt, was practiced humanely. Though such servants were considered chattel, they were not exploited as a labor force for profit and could buy their freedom. These serfs usually worked on temple lands or on the properties and households of the elite.

Agriculture was considered the noblest of professions; accordingly, farmers belonged to their own elite caste (*Goyigama*). Villages were usually concentrated close to irrigation tanks to enable easy access to water for agriculture. Their houses were located immediately below the tank bund, between the tank and the fields.

Elephants and horses were status symbols and could be afforded only by the nobility. The skills needed to train and care for these animals were regarded highly.

Rice, the staple food, was supplemented with other staples such as millet, yams, and vegetables. Food was preserved by roasting, sun-drying, burying in sand, and heat-drying over the kitchen hearth.

ART

While the *Mahavamsa* tells us that buildings were extensively painted and decorated, few traces of these remain today. The Sigiriya frescoes, dating from about AD 482, are the oldest surviving paintings from the Anuradhapura period. These paintings offer a rare glimpse of ancient Sinhala art at its zenith. The bold representations of well-formed bodies, ample bosoms, and full lips are unusually provocative. They show a maturity of style and sophistication of execution rarely seen in art of this vintage anywhere else in the world. These paintings are uniquely Sri Lankan in their character, and they are the only open display of female sensuality depicted in Sri Lankan art. These frescoes bear a strong resemblance to paintings in the Ajanta Caves in Maharashtra in India from about the same period, but the Sigiriya Frescoes are more colorful, vibrant, and fluid than those in India.

Traces of paintings have also been found on the walls and ceilings of many dagobas and vahalkadas that suggest that these were decorated extensively. Unfortunately, modern-day excavation and subsequent exposure to the elements led to the destruction of many of these paintings. Some fragments of color can still be seen on the vahalkadas and molding at the Ruwanwelisaya and Mirisawetiya dagobas.

Frescoe (circa AD 485) painted on the western rock-face at Sigiriya during the reign of King Kasyapa over one thousand five hundred years ago show the gracefulness of form unprecedented in art to this time. The subject matter of these paintings has been hotly debated. It is most likely that they are the ladies of King Kasyapa's harem depicted as heavenly beings, Apsaras, floating on a graceful cloud.

SCULPTURE

Sculpture during this period was predominantly of religious themes. Very few examples of secular sculptures such as those of kings or great battles exist.

Ancient stone carvers were constrained by the lack of soft, durable stone, such as sandstone and marble. The rock available locally was predominantly granite and gneiss, both very hard substances. For this reason, there was a meager output of rock sculpture in the early Anuradhapura period. With the invention of steel implements capable of working these hard surfaces in about the fifth century, there was a prolific growth in sculpture.

Many of the carvings around the vahalkadas of most dagobas, such as the pot of plenty and snake guardians, date back to the time of the original construction of these buildings.

The Isurumuniya Lovers, which dates from about the fourth century, is one of the earlier Gupta styles of carvings. The Samadhi Buddha statue, numerous moonstones, and guardstones such as those at the Abhayagiri Vihara are examples of masterful statue making of the Anuradhapura period, which reached its peak in the tenth century.

Toward the latter Anuradhapura period, there is a profusion of exquisite bronze cast statues of religious deities. Many of these were gilded and decorated with precious gems.

Dwarfs (gana) can often be seen supporting steps and temple walls. These jolly potbellied beings are associated with Kuvera, the god of wealth. Their significance and origins remain obscure (circa AD 650).

ഞാൻകരുതി വന്നവഴിയെപ്പൊയ്ക്കൊ
ള്ളാവതിഷ്ടം

LITERATURE

The earliest manifestations of writing are rock inscriptions written in Brāhmī script from the third century BC (the Brāhmī rock-cut "Edicts of Asoka" in India date to about the same time). This writing gradually evolved into the present-day Sinhala script. The Sinhala language is akin to Hindi, Bengali, and other Indo-Aryan tongues of North India. It is different from Tamil, the language of the people of South India.

As previously stated, the most extensive body of surviving literature comprises the religious texts and commentaries known as the *Dipavamsa*, *Mahavamsa*, and Culavamsa, written between the fifth and thirteenth centuries in Pali, an extinct Indo-Aryan language, by scholarly monks of the Mahavihara. Spanning a period of more than two thousand five hundred years, it is the oldest and longest authenticated chronicle of any country's history in the world.

The first uniquely Sinhala literature is graffiti scribbled on the Mirror Wall at Sigiriya. Written between the sixth and thirteenth centuries, these poems extol the virtues of the maidens of the Sigiriya Frescoes.

The oldest surviving Sinhala book, the *Siyabaslakara*, was written in the ninth or tenth century. It is based on an older Sanskrit work called the *Kavyadarsha* and deals with the art of writing poetry.

Left Sigiriya Graffiti (6-8th century).

Above: Brāhmī inscription at Vessagiriya (circa 3rd century BC).

The girl with the golden skin enticed the mind and eyes.
Ladies like you make men pour out their hearts
And you also have thrilled the body
Making it stiffen with desire.

(Sigiriya Graffiti)

Wet with cool dew drops
fragrant with perfume from the flowers
came the gentle breeze
jasmine and water lily
dance in the spring sunshine
side-long glances
of the golden hued ladies
stab into my thoughts
heaven itself cannot take my mind
as it has been captivated by one lass
among the five hundred I have seen here.

(Sigiriya Graffiti)

PART 3 - THE SITE

INTRODUCTION

The ancient precinct of the city of Anuradhapura is now a sacred site and a place of pilgrimage for millions of Buddhists. The Sri Maha Bodhi, Lovamahapaya, Ruwanwelisaya, Thuparama, Abhayagiri, Jetavanarama, Mirisawetiya, and Lankarama, in particular, are eight places of worship referred to as *Atamasthana*. Buddhist belief holds that these places were visited by the Buddha during his three visits to the country. For this reason, many of these structures have undergone extensive reconstruction and restoration.

Visitors should be respectful of the religious nature of the site and should dress and behave accordingly. Local pilgrims always dress in white and remove their headgear and footwear when visiting these sites.

The city of Anuradhapura was, for nearly one thousand five hundred years, a great monastic center as well as a royal capital. It was a fortified city with embankments, walls, moats, and four gates with wide boulevards leading to them. The distance from the north to the south gate was four gavuvas, about eight kilometers. Magnificent multistoried palaces and monasteries roofed in brilliant bronze or multicolored glazed tiles, and great dagobas soared majestically into the air. It also had gardens, parks, bathing ponds, a sophisticated sewerage system, and hospitals.

The inner city contained the palace and the administrative building. The outer city occupied an area of about twenty-one square kilometers. The main monastic complexes were located in the north and south. The main water reservoirs (referred to locally as tanks) were situated in the west and east. A large suburban population lived beyond the bunds (dykes) of these reservoirs, and beyond these were the agricultural lands. At its zenith, the city may have had a population in excess of two hundred thousand people. Surpluses in agriculture and the general prosperity of the populace supported a large population of officials, monks, artisans, traders, and scholars. Faxian, a Chinese chronicler visiting Anuradhapura in AD 411, noted that the streets were well maintained, smooth, and level with four principal avenues through the city. The main street, called the Ceremonial Street or Mangala Vithiya, started at the southern gate near the Thuparama. Faxian further notes that wealthy merchants of Indian, Mediterranean, and Persian origin and Sinhalese nobles lived in richly adorned houses. Multistory buildings, oil lamp-lit streets, ponds, baths, and parks supplied by water piped underground, and an efficient sewerage system flushed using recycled water also existed. Various kings such as King Buddhadasa (AD 337-365) and King Upa-tissa II (AD 522-524) built hospitals and hospices in the capital and throughout the kingdom.

Ancient buildings in Sri Lanka were constructed of wood, brick or granite usually plastered and painted in bright colors. Wooden structures in a tropical climate such as that of Sri Lanka perished rapidly. Brick, while far more durable, was also susceptible to the ravages of time and vegetation. Granite, on the other hand, was impervious to the elements, but being a very hard substance, it was very difficult to work with and not used in abundance. Unlike the ancient Greeks and Romans, Sri Lankan builders did not have a ready supply of sandstone or marble, materials far easier to quarry and work with.

Anuradhapura is a city dominated by dagobas, also referred to as stupas, cetiyas, and thūpas. These colossal structures, sitting in the center of a courtyard, usually enshrined a sacred relic of the Buddha or were built on a site of special significance. Surrounding these dagobas were massive monastic complexes belonging to the Mahavihara, Abhayagiri and Jetavana fraternities, each housing thousands of monks. Monastic complexes also had huge pools and ponds for bathing and ornamentation. These were supplied with water through underground piping from adjacent reservoirs such as the Tissa Wewa and Nuwara Wewa.

The ruins of the Mahavihara are least visible today because of the malicious destruction of its property during numerous religious upheavals and also, in more recent times, by the encroachment of the modern city of Anuradhapura over the ruins of the ancient Mahavihara site.

The ruins of the Abhayagiri complex located on the north side of the capital are the most extensive. In its heyday, it was the largest of seventeen monasteries located in the city.

The ruins of the Jetavana complex located on the south side of the capital are the most recent.

Mihintale
248 BC

Mihintale is a collection of small mountains approximately thirteen kilometers east of the city of Anuradhapura. These mountains were originally known as Missaka Pabbata and subsequently called Cetiyagiri or Chetiyapabbata, both meaning "The Mountain of Stupas."

It was here, on the full moon day in June 248 BC, that King Devanampiya-tissa (247–207 BC) came upon a hermit who addressed him thusly: "recluses we are, O great King, disciples of the King of Dharma." Having put the king at ease, the monk preached the new Dharma to the king. The king converted to Buddhism here and this place is considered the birthplace of Buddhism in Sri Lanka. It is from this encounter that its present name is derived: Mihintale—Mahinda's Mountain.

From these humble beginning, Mihintale grew to be the third-largest monastic complex in Sri Lanka. Faxian noted in AD 411 that there were two thousand monks living on the mountain. Initially, the monks of Mihintale were affiliated with the Mahavihara and its Theravada doctrine, but this changed with the great schism of the fourth century, and this monastery then became affiliated with the Abhayagiri fraternity and Mahayana doctrine of Buddhism.

Devanampiya-tissa (247–207 BC) furnished sixty-eight caves here for use by Mahinda's disciples. Elara (145–101 BC) visited and made an offering to the monks residing here. At the base of the mountain are the ruins of an ancient hospital built by Sena II (AD 851–885) with an interesting stone bath used to immerse a patient in a medicinal oils. An ancient stairway lined with frangipani trees 122 meters in length with 1840 steps leads to the first level and the main refectory containing two large stone food troughs measuring seven meters each. Another narrower flight of steps then leads to a structure flanked by two huge slabs inscribed by Mahinda IV (AD 956–972), setting out the code of governance of this monastery. Climbing one more level and to the east are the ruins of the Khantika Chatiya dagoba. We do not know who built it, but we first hear of it when Lanja-tissa (59–50 BC) refurbished it.

To the left of the Khantika Chatiya dagoba is a large cave through which one reaches yet more caves. It has been suggested that it is here that Kanirajanu-tissa (AD 89–92) had sixty monks who attempted to assassinate him thrown off a cliff.

The first 1840 steps leading up to Mihintale hill.

Ambasthale Dagoba and its enclosing vatadage pillars stands on the very spot were Mahinda questioned King Devanampiya-tissa with the riddle of the mango tree hence its name the Mango Tree Dagoba. The original dagoba was built here by Kutakanna-tissa (AD 16–38) and subsequently refurbished and rebuilt many times over. The Buddha statue is a recent addition.

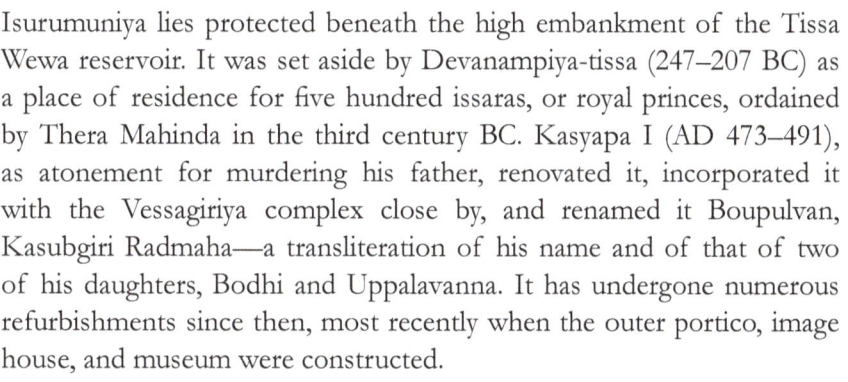

ISURUMUNIYA
248 BC

Isurumuniya lies protected beneath the high embankment of the Tissa Wewa reservoir. It was set aside by Devanampiya-tissa (247–207 BC) as a place of residence for five hundred issaras, or royal princes, ordained by Thera Mahinda in the third century BC. Kasyapa I (AD 473–491), as atonement for murdering his father, renovated it, incorporated it with the Vessagiriya complex close by, and renamed it Boupulvan, Kasubgiri Radmaha—a transliteration of his name and of that of two of his daughters, Bodhi and Uppalavanna. It has undergone numerous refurbishments since then, most recently when the outer portico, image house, and museum were constructed.

The Isurumuniya complex once occupied an area of about twenty hectares and was surrounded by moats and walls. To its right was Ranmasu Uyana, the Royal Gardens, and on its left was Vessagiriya.

The temple abuts a rock formation and consists of a small enclosed structure attached to the rock face. The structure sits on white stone slabs that serve as steps and rises above ground level. A stairway with two guardstones leads up to a nondescript Kandyan-style portico into the temple. The entranceway, chiseled into the rock, consists of carved columns with capitals that lead into an inner set of columns surmounted by a well-articulated archway. This is decorated with a relief of two mythological creatures known as Makaras, customarily found near statues of the Buddha. At the very center of the temple is a square chamber hewn deep into solid rock. In it is a statue of a seated Buddha, hewn out of the rock, meditating among the scented flower offerings. This statue is flanked by two standing statues made of wood. The chamber and statues have been painted in recent times.

A number of bas-reliefs are found carved into the rock outside the temple. To the right is a seventh-century carving of a man seated in a royal pose (maharajalila), his horse peering over his right shoulder. This has baffled archeologists, seeming out of place and having no significance in Buddhism. Carved into the opposite rock face is a niche that might have held a statue, now lost. Below this, near the waterline, are carvings of elephants frolicking by the water.

Isurumuniya temple; the bathing elephants are visible near the waterline and the man and his horse are visible below the roof-line.

A new image house to the left of the rock temple encloses a cave where Thera Mahinda himself might have reposed. It contains a number of recent statues that offer visitors an interesting opportunity to compare art past and present.

The museum building to the left of the image house contains a number of carvings and sculptures, the most famous being the Isurumuniya Lovers.

The Isurumuniya Lovers is a Gupta-style stone carving of an amorous couple, the woman seated on the man's lap, holding two fingers up in coy protestation at his flirtatiousness. A romanticized interpretation of this sculpture is that it depicts King Dutugamunu's son Saliya, who surrendered his right to the throne for the love of a low-caste maiden named Asokamala. Another is that it is a depiction of the deities Shiva and Parvathi. A fresh interpretation is that it is a composite image drawing from many sources. It is mostly likely that this fifth-century Gupta-style carving was commissioned by King Kasyapa I as part of his refurbishment of Isurumuniya and Vessagiriya. The sculptor is probably depicting Saliya and Asokamala but using the painting of "two lovers" found in the Ajanta Caves in Maharashtra India as his inspiration. This, in turn, might be based on a much older iconographic depiction of Siva and Parvathi, who are often portrayed similarly, with Parvathi seated on Siva's knee.

Vessagiriya
248 BC

The Vessagiriya complex, with its numerous rock formations scooped out and hollowed into little caves and cells for meditating, lies mostly in ruin today. Close to present-day Isurumuniya, it is often overshadowed by its more famous neighbor. It was here that five hundred vaisyas (those of the third caste, usually traders and craftsmen) resided after their conversion to Buddhism by Thera Mahinda in the third century BC. Hence it was known as Vaisya-giri, which in time became Vessagiriya. It was also close to the Vessagiriya forest to which King Vattagamani-abhaya (44–44 BC) fled during his hasty retreat from the capital, Anuradhapura, in 44 BC and where he befriended the Thera Mahā-tissa to whom he would later bequeath Abhayagiri Vihara. King Kasyapa I (AD 478–496) merged Vessagiriya with Isurumuniya, extensively refurbished them both, and renamed this new monastery Boupulvan-Kasubgiri-Radmaha, transliterating his name and those of two of his daughters, Bodhi and Uppalavanna. The Sangha refused to accept his gift because the king was a parricide, having murdered his father. A compromise was reached where the refurbished complex was donated to the Buddha and therefore acceptable the Sangha.

The history of Vessagiriya predates the Anuradhapura Kingdom, showing evidence of early occupancy by Veddas, the aboriginal people of Sri Lanka. The are was subsequently occupied by forest-dwelling monks who resided here and sustained themselves by seeking alms. Over the entrance of many of these caves are drip ledges incised into the rock surface to prevent rain water from flowing into the caves. Some caves bear the names of those who donated them to the clergy. The smoothed rock floors of some caves is evidence of thousands of years of occupancy, the rock having many concave depressions after being rubbed smooth by year upon year of sitting. Some caves were once plastered and contain the remnants of colorful and elaborate frescoes.

An impromptu shrine in a cave at Vessagiriya

THUPARAMA
250 BC

The Thuparama was the first dagoba built in the country and the oldest building of the Mahavihara. Since it was the only dagoba (thupa) at the time, its name was formed by the concatenation of two ancient Sanskrit words: thupa (stupa) and arama (monastery). Constructed in about 250 BC by King Devanampiya-tissa, it is said to enshrine the right collarbone of the Buddha. It was originally built in the shape of a heap of paddy (rice before threshing or in the husk).

The four concentric rows of graceful stone pillars of diminishing height which once numbered 176 (only 43 are still standing) surround the dagoba, and supported a circular roof known as a vatadage. This vatadage is believed to have been constructed by King Gothabhaya (AD 309–322). There is much controversy about the shape of the Vatadage. Some suggest that the entire dagoba was covered by a domed vatadage. This, however, is very improbable, for the pillars are too delicate to support a heavy dome. Furthermore, the concept of a dome was not known to local architects of this time. It is more likely that the vatadage was a covered structure whose gently sloping roof had an open center from which the upper portion of the dagoba might have protruded. By the seventh century the dagoba was in ruins and was restored by Aggabodhi II (AD 601–611).

The dagoba, once decorated extensively in gold and silver with many of its fitments studded with precious gems, was so opulent that it was looted many times. In light of its special significance, it was also rebuilt numerous times, but in the tenth century, South Indian Cholas plundered the entire three-acre complex, leading to its final abandonment.

The current bell shape of the Thuparama dates to its reconstruction in AD 1862. Measured from the platform, it is nineteen meters tall and has a diameter of eighteen meters. The platform is paved with blocks of granite.

An exquisitely carved Nagaraja Guardstone at the entrance to Thuparama.

Top. The undulating rim of this stone trough produced numerous rivulets of water for devotees to cleanse themselves before entering the premises.

Sacred Sri Maha Bodhi tree
250 BC

The Sri Maha Bodhi, the Most Resplendent Bodhi Tree, or Jaya Siri Maha Bodin Vahansa, is central to Buddhist religion in Sri Lanka and is the key inspiration around which Anuradhapura flourished. It was grown from a sapling of the original tree (Ficus religiosa) under which Prince Siddhartha Gautama attained supreme enlightenment and became the Buddha. It is the most venerated of all Buddhist places of worship. Nearly two thousand three hundred years old, the Bodhi tree is the oldest historically authenticated tree in the world. Planted in about 240 BC on a high terrace in the royal Mahameghavana Park, it was a gift from the Mauryan Emperor Asoka to the first Buddhist ruler of Sri Lanka, Devanampiya-tissa (247–207 BC). Since its initial planting twenty-three centuries ago, it has been faithfully tended to, even after the city was abandoned in AD 1012, by an uninterrupted succession of guardian monks and local villages known as Villidura. To safeguard the Bodhi tree from roaming wild elephants, its caretakers used to light bonfires around it each night. The vast quantity of firewood required was supplied each August during the full moon by local villagers, who saw this as their sacred duty. As time passed, people started calling this the Daramiti (Firewood Bundle) Perehera, and it continues as an annual ritual to this day. The present wall was constructed during the reign of King Kirthi Sri Rajasingha (AD 1743–1751) to protect it from roaming wild elephants, and the gold-colored railing was added in 1966. The parent tree from which this sapling was obtained no longer exists in India, having been chopped down by anti-Buddhist religious fanatics when Buddhism fell into disfavor in India. The Bodhi tree in Sri Lanka has been more fortunate, never having been attacked during the numerous occasions when Anuradhapura was plundered. However, it hasn't survived totally unscathed. In 1907 and 1911, two of its branches fell off during rainstorms, and in 1929, a madman chopped an entire branch off the sacred tree.

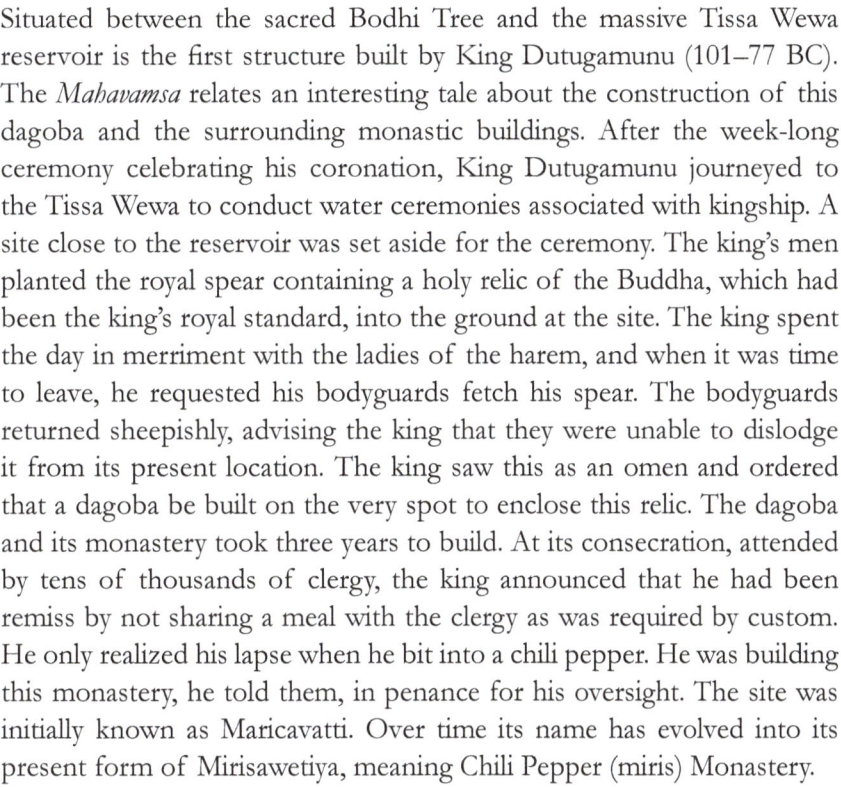

Mirisawetiya
101 BC

Situated between the sacred Bodhi Tree and the massive Tissa Wewa reservoir is the first structure built by King Dutugamunu (101–77 BC). The *Mahavamsa* relates an interesting tale about the construction of this dagoba and the surrounding monastic buildings. After the week-long ceremony celebrating his coronation, King Dutugamunu journeyed to the Tissa Wewa to conduct water ceremonies associated with kingship. A site close to the reservoir was set aside for the ceremony. The king's men planted the royal spear containing a holy relic of the Buddha, which had been the king's royal standard, into the ground at the site. The king spent the day in merriment with the ladies of the harem, and when it was time to leave, he requested his bodyguards fetch his spear. The bodyguards returned sheepishly, advising the king that they were unable to dislodge it from its present location. The king saw this as an omen and ordered that a dagoba be built on the very spot to enclose this relic. The dagoba and its monastery took three years to build. At its consecration, attended by tens of thousands of clergy, the king announced that he had been remiss by not sharing a meal with the clergy as was required by custom. He only realized his lapse when he bit into a chili pepper. He was building this monastery, he told them, in penance for his oversight. The site was initially known as Maricavatti. Over time its name has evolved into its present form of Mirisawetiya, meaning Chili Pepper (miris) Monastery.

The dagoba's base, which is fifty-one meters in diameter today, was originally sixty-one meters. Its most noteworthy feature is the beautiful vahalkadas found at the four cardinal points of the dagoba. A number of other ruins lie scattered about the compound, including a large rice trough, a dining hall, and a chapter house.

The complex has undergone numerous renovations during its long life, in the course of which its original shape has been lost. The present restoration was completed in 1993.

A building plan etched on a stone slab, believed to be that of this monastery, can be seen at the Anuradhapura Archeological Museum.

LOVAMAHAPAYA – THE BRAZEN PALACE
98 BC

The Lovamahapaya is an enigma. Why was such an opulent complex occupied by monks aspiring to a life of piety, poverty and prayer? Some have suggested that it was meant to test their fortitude by reminding them of the material world they had to forfeit in order to reach true enlightenment. Others suggest it was a reflection of the lavish lifestyle the monks of the Mahavihara had grown accustomed to.

Originally built of wood, it was a gift from King Dutugamunu (101–77 BC) to the Mahavihara. The *Mahavamsa*, which is usually scant in its praise of material things, waxes lyrical about it, telling us that this nine-story building was forty-five meters tall and forty-five meters to a side, and that its colorful exterior and bronze roof tiles made it dazzle in the sunlight, earning it the name of Brazen Palace. We are told that its windows were made of silver. Its coral balustrades were decked with gems and surrounded by rows of little silver bells. Vivid scenes from the Jataka tales were painted on the walls. All its furnishings were of the most exquisite kind: its crockery was made of gold, and even the pillars were embedded with gems. The building was said to contain one thousand chambers. Even allowing for hyperbole, the building must have been "brazen" indeed. The lowest floors were reserved for the novice monks. The next level was for the monks who knew Tripitaka. The levels above that were for the monks who had achieved Sovan, Sakurdagami, and Anagami. The uppermost levels were for the monks who had reached the state of Arhath.

Just seven years after its construction, an accidentally tipped oil lamp destroyed the magnificent Lovamahapaya. Saddha-tissa (77–59 BC) rebuilt it to a less grandiose seven stories. It was later restored to five stories by Sirinaga II (AD 300–302). Jettha-tissa I (AD 323–333) again raised it to seven stories. Mahasena (AD 334–362) completely demolished it and donated its material to the Abhayagiri Vihara. His son, Sirimeghavanna (AD 362–390), rebuilt it only to see it plundered during a Pandyan invasion from India. It was rebuilt once more by Sena II (AD 851–985) only to be ransacked by a Cola invasion from South India in the tenth century and was abandoned.

King Parakramabahu of the Polonnaruwa Kingdom rebuilt it in AD 1156. It is at this point that we first hear of the sixteen hundred pillars that are on the site today. The pillars are a motley lot, consisting of rough-hewn posts, columns with tenons, and others planted upside-down, their rough-hewn bases exposed. The foundation stones, too, appear to be from a number of older structures. It appears that the materials for this structure were scavenged by Parakramabahu's builders from other ruins around the city.

Ruwanwelisaya
80 BC

The Ruwanwelisaya, also known as Mahathupa, Swarnamali Chaitya, and Rathnamali, is the most venerated dagoba in Sri Lanka. Its present name is derived from the Sinhala words for gem (*ruwan*) and sand (*weli*). The dagoba owes much of its popularity to its being built by King Dutugamunu, a national hero of the Sinhalese people who built it to celebrate his victory over the usurper Elara.

The Ruwanwelisaya has a bubble shape and, at a height of ninety-two meters, is as tall as a thirty-story building. Its base has a diameter of ninety-one meters and a circumference of 292 meters; it is the third largest brick structure in the world. It sits on an elevated, paved square platform. The outside perimeter of this platform is decorated with a frieze of elephants that appear as though they are carrying the weight of the dagoba on their backs. Four stairways facing north, south, east, and west lead up to this platform from a courtyard below. Facing these stairways are four ornamental façades called vahalkadas (frontispieces.) The dagoba itself sits on a shallow plinth referred to as a "Weli Konda," a feature found in very large dagobas. Above the Weli Konda are three concentric "pesava" terraces of diminishing size, placed atop each other. Flower offerings were once placed on these pesavas. The solid white bubble-shaped dome appears to sits atop the pesava rings. Embedded deep within this dome was a small chamber said to contain a number of relics of the Buddha. On top of the hemispheric dome is a solid square structure known as a Hatharaskotuwa. This is topped with a spire. At the base of the spire is a band called a Devathakotuwa in which are embedded statues of various gods. Above this is a tapered spire made of decreasing concentric circles, at the pinnacle of which is a gem. Initially this was said to have been a bubble-shaped ruby as large as a man's fist, but this has long since been looted.

In ancient times the Hatharaskotuwa was a railed enclosure with an octagonal column supporting one or more symbolic umbrellas, typically solid discs called a chathra (an example of this style can be seen in the Sanchi Dagoba in India). It was customary for kings to mount their own smaller chathra atop an existing one, thus eventually creating a multitude of chathras. Over time this arrangement became impractical and structurally unsound and was replaced by a solid Hatharaskotuwa with a spire.

The author of the *Mahavamsa* dedicates three chapters to the construction of this dagoba, and understandably so—this is the largest and most significant dagoba of the Mahavihara to which he belonged. The detailed account of its construction provides an invaluable insight into its construction and into the king who built it. If not for the *Mahavamsa*, the builder of this dagoba, like those of so many other structures of the Anuradhapura Kingdom, would have been lost to history. The *Mahavamsa*, in recounting its construction, freely intermingles fact and fiction to create a rich legend.

Considering the sanctity of his endeavor, King Dutugamunu resolved to build his dagoba without burdening the people with any additional taxes. He also decreed that no forced labor would be employed. He was intent on building this dagoba entirely of his own resources. It is believed that it cost King Dutugamunu six and a half million coins paid in wages as well as for food, clothing, and other amenities that he provided his workers. According to the *Mahavamsa*, the materials required for this vast undertaking were surreptitiously provided by the gods. But by stripping away the hyperbole, one may be able to postulate that on unifying the entire country, Dutugamunu acquired a large revenue base and was fortunate in that large new deposits of copper, gold, and silver were also discovered during this period. The *Mahavamsa* describes how the foundation of the Ruwanwelisaya was laid: First the land was dug out to a depth of six meters down to bedrock. Then crushed stones were laid and stamped down by elephants whose feet were bound in leather boots. Then butter clay; a slurry made of clay, an adhesive made from the resin of the Wood Apple tree [Feronia Elephantum], and sweetened water [from coconuts], was spread over the stones and bricks laid over the clay. Over these a rough cement and then a layer of cinnabar [possibly red mercury sulfide] was laid; on top of this a network of iron was laid; over this a layer of mountain crystal, then more stone, all bound together with butter clay. Finally, a copper sheeting eight inches thick was laid and, over this a sheet of silver seven inches thick [this might be an exaggeration] soaked in a solution of arsenic dissolved in sesame oil was laid. This more or less provided the ancient builders with a reinforced concrete foundation, complete with moisture proofing, on which the superstructure was to be built. Vast quantities of baked brick were used, with very thin layers of butter clay applied between each layer. The use of this thin layer of clay meant that each brick was in direct contact with its neighbor and provided stronger compression strength. The materials used in dagoba construction were subjected to strict quality control. We are told, for example, how a pious monk tried to have a brick he manufactured himself installed in the dagoba so as to gain himself extra religious merit. Upon hearing of this, the king had the brick found and removed and the offending monk admonished for his misguided piety. (Another monk did, however, succeed in installing a brick that could not be removed.) The outer surface was waterproofed using a layer of nine to ten inches of lime concrete plaster. The dagoba, whitewashed, gleamed white with a paint mixture made of nearly nine tons of lime, water, salt, and sago (a starch extracted from the pith of the Metroxylon sagu palm)—the sago improved the consistency and adhesion of the paint to the plaster surface.

The *Mahavamsa* informs us that sacred relics of the Buddha were housed within the dome of the Ruwanwelisaya. The

relic chamber roof was constructed using six large translucent stone slabs called "Medakavan," imported from India. This allowed sunlight to illuminate the chamber from above, casting a soft light. Inside this chamber was a Bodhi tree nine meters tall with five branches constructed of silver and encrusted with precious jewels. The roots were made of coral imported from Arabia and rested on a surface encrusted with sapphires. Over it, on the border of a beautiful canopy, was a network of pearl bells and chains of little golden bells. From the four corners of the canopy hung bundles of pearl strings. The figures of Sun, Moon, and stars and of different lotus flowers made of jewels were fastened to the canopy, and a golden statue of the Buddha placed beneath it. The fingernails and whites of the eyes were made of mountain crystal; the palms of the hands, soles of the feet, and lips of red coral; the eyebrows and pupils of sapphires; and the teeth of diamonds. Surrounding the statue were many gold figures representing events and characters from the Buddha's life. The walls of the relic chamber were painted with events from the story of the Buddha. The sacred relics, it is said, were brought from the "Naga World"—whose residents might have been the last custodians of Buddha's relics on mainland India, where Buddhism was on the decline.

The Ruwanwelisaya has undergone many reconstructions since its initial construction. King Lanja-tissa (59–50 BC) faced the terraces with limestone blocks. Khallata-naga (50–44 BC) constructed the sand courtyard (Valimaluwa) surrounding the raised platform. Cora-naga (3 BC–AD 9) enlarged the sand courtyard and paved it with ornamental stones. Siri-naga I (AD 249–268) reconstructed and gilded the umbrella. Dhatusena (AD 460–478) restored and gilded the umbrella and embellished it with precious stones. Mahanaga (AD 556–559) built the elephant frieze and renovated the paintings. Aggabodhi I (AD 568–601) installed an umbrella of stone. Moggallana III (AD 611–617) renovated the dagoba. Parakramabahu 1 (AD 1153–1186) restored the dagoba to its original height and installed a new spire. Nissankamalla (AD 1187–1196) carried out repairs and erected a stone replica of the dagoba on the platform. The most recent reconstruction was carried out in the late twentieth century. The two-foot-high rock crystal that surmounts the spire today was donated by the people of Myanmar.

Abhayagiri Dagoba
44 BC

Abhayagiri Dagoba is the second largest dagoba in the world and is one of the eight holiest Buddhist shrines. It was built in 44 BC by King Vattagamani-abhaya. It was for many years misidentified as being the Jetavana Dagoba. It had a hemispherical "paddy heap"–shaped (paraboloid) dome, which the ancient engineers determined to be the most stable shape for a brick structure of such a colossal size. Oriented along north-south and east-west axes, it was originally 123 meters high, with a circumference of 344 meters. The boundary walls are within 1.5 degrees of true orientation, and the top of the spire is only twenty-three millimeters off dead center with its base. The dagoba was plastered with a thick coat of lime mortar, parts of which are still visible today. As was the custom, it was painted in gleaming white. The relics of the Buddha are said to have been enshrined within a figurine of a bull made of gold. When the Tooth Relic was brought to Sri Lanka in the fourth century, Abhayagiri was selected to house it during public veneration until the end of the collapse of the Anuradhapura Kingdom.

It was renovated by King Gajabahu (AD 114–136) and again by King Parakramabahu (AD 1153–1186). The current height of the structure is much less than that of the original. This modern-day reconstruction, completed in 2012, follows the form of the dagoba as rebuilt by King Parakramabahu.

During restoration work carried out by the British in 1887, a tunnel was dug approximately thirty-two meters above the eastern entrance of the dagoba to its center, a distance of fifty-two meters. Then a vertical shaft was dug down to the base. No valuables were found; only a few minor artifacts embedded during the dagoba's construction were uncovered. Further investigations also discovered that the dagoba had been penetrated in earlier times and these tunnels subsequently filled with inferior building materials. Any treasures that the dagoba might have held appear to have been plundered many centuries ago.

Samadhi Buddha
AD 300

The Samadhi Buddha statue is considered one of the finest in Sri Lanka. It is a two-and-a-half-meter-tall sculpture of the Buddha in the Samadhi posture, with the Buddha sitting cross-legged with upturned palms, placed one over the other, on his lap.

Sculpted from dolomite marble, sometime between the third and fifth centuries in the Gupta style, it is believed to have been one of four that were positioned around a bodhigara or Bodhi-tree shine. Traces of paint found under the right shoulder suggest that it might have been painted.

It is claimed that the face of the statue possesses three different dispositions depending on the angle from which it is viewed. When observed slightly off center from the left, the face seems to wear a sad expression. When viewed from the right, it shows a somewhat happier disposition. When viewed directly, it exudes a serene, meditative presence.

The statue was found in 1886, lying abandoned on the forest floor. It had suffered some damage, most noticeably to its nose. It was set upright on a temporary pedestal and the nose reconstructed; some say this reconstruction was very poorly done. In 1914, the statue was damaged by treasure hunters and was repaired once more.

BISO MALIGAYA: THE QUEEN'S PALACE
AD 650

Known today as Biso Maligaya, or the Queen's Palace, due to the belief that this is the monastery built by Vattagamani-abhaya (29–17 BC) as restitution to his second wife Somadevi on her return from captivity in India in around 29 BC, this complex of five buildings was actually a monastic compound. The central multistoried residence of the chief monk contains an image room with a lotus pedestal on which once stood a statue, now lost. At its front entrance is a famous moonstone, or sandakada pahana. This moonstone is believed to date from the seventh or eighth century and is one of the most exquisite examples of an entrance moonstone in existence today.

The concept of the moonstone is believed to have been borrowed from India. Local artisans, however, progressively fashioned them with uniquely Sri Lankan motifs. Initially these were inconsequential in their design, but at the height of the Anuradhapura Kingdom, they had evolved into highly stylized, richly decorated, and remarkably uniform works of art.

A moonstone, made of a semicircular slab of granite or gneiss was usually placed at the entrance of important religious buildings. It was carved with concentric motifs of fire, animals, plants, geese, and lotus petals. The outermost ring with its fire motif represented desire and the pain associated with it. The next pattern consisted of the repeated occurrence of four animals—the lion, elephant, bull, and horse. One theory holds that these four animals represent the four noble truths of the Buddha; an alternate theory posits that they represent birth, illness, aging, and death—the endless cycle of Samsara, or rebirths. The next band consists of twisting vines and represents an ensnaring life force. The band after that consists of a string of geese, each holding a lotus sprig in its beak—a sign of wisdom, purity, wholeness, and goodness together with the ability to separate good from evil. Another arc of leaves and flowers follows, suggesting the heavenly worlds. After this level has been reached, one is capable of attaining Nirvana, represented here by the elevated high relief of the lotus motif.

The steps of this building are also home to a wholesome collection of little gargoyles.

Rathna Prasada: Jewel Palace
AD 227

The Rathna Prasada, or Jewel Palace, was constructed by Kanitthatissa (AD 227–245) for the head abbot of the Dhammaruci sect of the Abhayagiri monastery. The Mahavihara had its Brazen Palace, and Abhayagiri countered with its Jewel Palace. It was rebuilt by Mahinda II (772–792) and presented with a huge golden statue of Buddha. The building was looted many times. One such instance was during the reign of Sena I (AD 8321–851) when the Pandyan army stole the golden statue donated by Mahinda II. Sena II (AD 851-885) avenged this humiliation and restored it to much of its former glory. The *Mahavamsa* also tells us that a group of ascetic monks lived close by and by custom their place of refuge was a place of sanctuary. During the reign of Udaya III (AD 934–937), a number of his officials fled to the protection of this sanctuary.

The king's soldiers violated the sanctity of the refuge, entered the premises, and beheaded the offenders. The monks, dismayed by the defilement of their refuge, fled. The populace rose up in revolt, scaled the walls of the compound, and beheaded many of those responsible. The royal princes, who had also been party to this crime, feared for their lives, and sought out the monks and begged their forgiveness. The ascetics accepted the apology and returned to be greeted by the king, who also sought their forgiveness. From then on, the king governed with more restraint. Because of its massive pillars, this building was misidentified as the elephant stables, no consideration being given to its small entrances and stairs through which elephants would most certainly not have been able to pass.

The placement of guardstones (muragal) at entrances to buildings with protecting deities, such as found here, is a custom borrowed from Hinduism and demonstrates the influences of other religions and architectural traditions on local builders. The Nagaraja, or Snake King, is a humanized (anthropomorphic) portrayal of the King Cobra. They offer protection to the building and are regarded as symbols of fertility and masters of the underworld. In Buddhist belief, Nagaraja Muchalinda is said to have sheltered the meditating Buddha as he attained enlightenment.

The Nagaraja Guardstone found here dates from around the fifth century and was one of a pair placed at the base of the stairs of this building. It is the most exquisite surviving guardstone in all of Anuradhapura. The Nagaraja deity stands gracefully, the weight of his body resting on one foot. His composure is fluid, his garments lithe and light. He holds a flower stem and a pot of plenty (punkalasa) symbolizing fertility. He has a seven-hooded cobra headdress. At his feet is a gana, a jolly potbellied creature associated with Kuvera, the god of wealth and prosperity. Two mythical sea creatures known as Makaras form the base of an arch above the Nagaraja's head. They are seen disgorging lions and humans.

Pancavasa: Mahasena's Palace
AD 500

This rarely visited building, located behind the Rathna Prasada, contains a beautiful moonstone at its entrance. Often referred to as Mahasena's Palace, it was actually the principal residential unit and once had a large statue facing the entrance.

Burrows Pavilion
AD 300

This stone pavilion (now called the Burrows Pavilion in honor of the Englishman who restored it between 1884 and 1886) is thought to be the entrance to the oldest Bodhigara in the Abhayagiri Complex, where the Third Samadhi Statue is located.

Refectory: Monks' Dining Hall
AD 29

The Chinese traveler monk Faxian, who visited this monastery in the fifth century, noted approvingly that the monastery had five thousand resident monks. With so many monks to feed, it became impossible to sustain them by the usual Buddhist practice of begging for alms. As a result, a centralized system of almsgiving was implemented where donations were deposited at centralized collection points, and these, together with the produce from the monastery lands were used to feed the huge congregation of clergy. This dining facility measuring forty-two meters on each side is where the monks came to collect their midday meal. A sundial nearby was used for this purpose. The massive nineteen-meter stone trough with removable side panels for easy cleaning, constructed by King Aggabodhi II (AD 601–611) was used to hold rice to feed the monks. A smaller stone trough close by might have contained a side dish of curry or gruel. Monks who were entitled to eat at the refectory were issued wooden ration tickets.

ATH POKUNA: ELEPHANT POND
AD 300

The Elephant Pond is 159 meters long, 53 meters wide, and 9.5 meters deep. It has a capacity of 7.5 million liters, as much as six Olympic-sized swimming pools. The pond was used by the monks of the Abhayagiri monastery. Water was supplied to the pond via underground conduits from the nearby Periyamkulama reservoir.

Kuttam Pokuna: Twin Ponds
AD 575

The wealth and opulence of the Abhayagiri vihara is clearly evident in the fine workmanship of these bathing ponds. They are thought to have been built in around AD 575–608. The smaller, and older, northern pond is 28 meters long, and the larger pond is 40 meters long. They are 15.5 meters wide and 4.5 meters deep. The ponds have stepped sides, are lined with granite, and are interconnected via underground pipes. Water was supplied through these pipes, filtered through a number of filtration chambers before entering the ponds through a spigot shaped like a dragon's head. Water from both ponds drained via a small outlet in the smaller northern pond, and was channeled to irrigate rice fields close by. The steps leading down to the ponds are flanked by punkalas, or pots of plenty. A naga stone in very good condition is located next to the water spigot of the smaller pond.

JETHAWANARAMAYA
AD 360

The Jetavana Monastery was founded by King Mahasena (AD 334–362) and the Jetavanarama dagoba at the time of its construction was 122 meters tall making it the third tallest structure in the ancient world after the pyramids. It still holds the record for the largest brick structure in the world. Estimated to contain ninety-three million bricks it took twenty-seven years to complete. Standing on a platform of three hectares, it is one hundred meters in diameter. This means that over fifteen thousand bricks were laid each day. The kilns required to fire these bricks, the firewood burned, the mortar required to bind the bricks, etc. would have been a stupendous logistical feat for the builders of the third century. There are sufficient bricks in the Jetavanarama to build a wall forty-three kilometers long, seven meters high and one meter wide.

The foundation of the dagoba is nearly eight meters deep and sits on bedrock. Undulations in the bedrock were filled out with clay and leveled, and on this was built a two-tier brick platform. The cylindrical base of the dagoba sits on the topmost platform. The structure and building techniques used are very similar to those used to construct the Ruwanwelisaya and Abhayagiri dagobas.

Until the thirteenth century, Jetavana was said to enshrine a piece of belt (sash) of the Buddha.

The monastery associated with it once had more than three thousand Buddhist monks. Its ruins extend for kilometers around the dagoba.

Remains of Residence
AD 900–1000

The area south of the dagoba is littered with the ruins of the Jetavana monastery, which once housed 3000 monks. The initial monastery buildings were constructed north of the dagoba around the third century in an area that has remained largely unexcavated, and they expanded south and east until the tenth century, when Anuradhapura was abandoned.

Buddhist Railing
AD 900–1000

Immediately behind the Jetavana museum lies a latticed fence whose four entrances are oriented toward the cardinal points. It encloses an area of 42 meters by 34 meters at the center of which was an image house which has long since disappeared. The three tiers of the fence are said to represent Buddhism's "triple gems" (the Buddha, his teachings, and the Sangha).

BIBLIOGRAPHY

REFERENCES

Aiyangar, Krishnaswami S. Some Contributions Of South India To Indian Culture. Calcutta: The University Of Calcutta, 1923. Print.
Allan, J., H. H. Dodwell, and T. W. Haig. The Cambridge Shorter History of India. Delhi: Chand, 1969. Print.
Ariyadasa, Kalakeerthi E. "Sculpture of Man and Horse at Isurumuniya." The Archaeology News Network:. Daily News, 21 Aug. 212. Web. 19 July 2014.
Armstrong, Keith. India and Sri Lanka in the Time of the Roman Julio-Claudians. London: n.p., 2013. Print
Bandaranayake, Senake, and Gamini Jayasinghe. The Rock and Wall Paintings of Sri Lanka. Colombo: Lake House hop, 1986. Print.
Bandaranayake, Senake. Sinhalese Monastic Architecture: The Vihâras of Anurâdhapura. Leiden: Brill, 1974. Print.
Batemen-jones. An Illustrated Guide to the Buried Cities of Ceylon. Danbury: Asian Educational Services, 1994. Print.
Beal, Si-yu-ki, Buddhist Records of the Western World, transl. from the Chinese of Hiuen-thsang, ii, pp. 246-247 ;
Bhikkhu, Mettanando. "How the Buddha Died." Bangkok Post [Bangkok] 15 May 2001: n. pag. Print.
Bowden, Russell. "Sri Lanka's Earliest Libraries - Anuradhapura and Polonnuruwa Periods." Sri Lankan Journal of Librarianship and Information Management Sri Lankan J Librarianship and Info Mgt 4.3-4 (2012): n. pag. Web.
Cave, Henry William. The Ruined Cities of Ceylon: Illustrated with Photographs Taken by the Author in the Year 1896. London: Hutchinson &, 1907. Print.
Chakrabarti, Dilip K. The Geopolitical Orbits of Ancient India: the Geographical Frames of the Ancient Indian Dynasties. Oxford University Press, 2011.
Charles, Walker,. Wonders of the ancient world. London: Orbis, 1980. Print.
Codrington, Humphrey W. Short History of Ceylon. New Delhi: Asian Educational Services, 1994. Print.
Cowell, Edward B. The Jātaka, Or, Stories of the Buddha's Former Births. Oxford: Pali Text Society, 1995. Print.
Davey, John. An account of the interior of Ceylon, and of its inhabitants: with travels. London: Longman, Hurst, Orme, Rees & Bworn, 1821.
Davids, T. W. Rhys, and William Stede. The Pali Text Society's Pali-English Dictionary. London: Pali Text Society; Sole Agents Routledge & K. Paul, 1972. Print.
Davidson, Linda Kay. Pilgrimage from the Ganges to Graceland : an encyclopedia. Santa Barbara, Calif: ABC-CLIO, 2002. Print.
Dhammika, Shravasti, and Aśoka. The Edicts of King Asoka: An English Rendering. Kandy, Sri Lanka: Buddhist Publication Society, 1993. Print.
Dhammika, Shravasti, and Nānatusita. Sacred Island: A Buddhist Pilgrim's Guide to Sri Lanka. Kandy: Buddhist Publication Society, 2008. Print.
Farrer, Reginald. In Old Ceylon. London: Edward Arnold, 1908. Print.
Faxian, and James Legge. A Record of Buddhist Kingdoms: Being an Account by the Chinese Monk Faxian of His Travels in India and Ceylon (A.D. 399-414) in Search of the Buddhist Books of Discipline. New York: Paragon Book Reprint, 1965. Print.
Fernando Dennis N. Decline of the ancient Hydraulic civilization of Sri Lanka http://www.sangam.org/2010/01/Hydraulic_Civilisation.php?uid=3805
Fernando, Mithra. "The myth of 'Lion ancestry' & adults-only tales of the Lala land." Asian Tribune Internet Daily Newspaper. 21 July 2007.
Fernando, W. B. Marcus., and C. E. Godakumbura. Ancient City of Anuradhapura. Colombo: Archaeological Dept., 1965. Print.
Forbes, Jonathan, and George Turnour. Eleven Years in Ceylon. Comprising Sketches of the Field Sports and Natural History of That Colony, and an Account of Its History and Antiquities. London: R. Bentley, 1841. Print.
Geiger, Wilhelm, and Mabel H. Bode. The Mahavamsa or Great Chronicle of Ceylon. Colombo: Ceylon Government Information Department, 1960. Print.
Geiger, Wilhelm. "The Trustworthiness of the Mahavamsa." The Indian Historical Quarterly 6.2 (1930): 202-28.
Geiger, Wilhelm. Culavamsa Being The More Recent Part Of Mahavamsa 2 Vols. New Delhi: Asian Educational Services, 1998. Print. First Published in 1929.
Gooneskere, L. R. Buddhist Commentarial Literature. Kandy, Ceylon: Buddhist Publication Society, 1967. Print.
Gunasēkara, B. The Rājāvaliya: Or, A Historical Narrative of Sinhalese Kings from Vijaya to Vimala Dharma Sūriya II, to Which Are Added a Glossary and a List of Sovereigns. Colombo: Govt. Printer, 1954. Print.
Gunawardana, R. A. L. H. The People of the Lion - The Sinhala Identity and Ideology in History and Historiography. Ceylon: U of Peradeniya, 1979. Print.
Harischandra, Walisinha. The Scared City of Anuradhapura. New Delhi: Asian Educational Services, 1998. Print.
Herath, H. M. Mervyn. Monarchs of Sri Lanka. Sarasavi Bookshop, 2003. Print.
Holt, John. The Sri Lanka Reader: History, Culture, Politics. Durham: Duke UP, 2011. Print.
Hulugalle, H. A. J. Ceylon of the Early Travellers. Colombo: Printed at the Wesley, 1969. Print.
Inden, Ronald B., Jonathan S. Walters, and Daud Ali. Querying the Medieval: Texts and the History of Practices in South Asia. Oxford: Oxford UP, 2000. Print.
Indicopleustes, Cosmas. "CH XI - A Description of Indian Animals, and of the Island of Taprobane." Christian Topography. 550. 358-73. Print.
Jaques, Tony. Dictionary of Battles and Sieges Bind 1-3. a Guide to 8,500 Battles from Antiquity through the Twenty-first Century: A-E. N.p.: n.p., 2007. Print.
Jouveau-Dubreuil, Gabriel, and Svaminadha Dikshita V. S. The Pallavas. Pondicherry: Author, 1917. Print.
Karunaratne, L. K. "The History of Buddhist Architecture in Sri Lanka." Digital Library & Museum of Buddhist Studies. N.p., 1998. Web. 4 Aug. 2012.
Kirk, R. L. "The Legend of Prince Vijaya — a Study of Sinhalese Origins." American Journal of Physical Anthropology 45.1 (1976): 91-99. Print.
Knighton, William. The History of Ceylon from the Earliest Period to the Present Time. New York: Adamant Media Corporation, 2005. Print.
Knox, Robert. An Historical Relation of the Island Ceylon, in the East-Indies Together, with an Account of the Detaining in Captivity the Author and Divers Other Englishmen Now Living There, and of the Authors Miraculous Escape : Illustrated with Figures, and a Map of the Island. London: Printed by Richard Chiswell ..., 1681. Print.
Kshatriya, Gautam Kumar. "Genetic affinities of Sri Lankan populations - page 5 | Human Biology." Bnet Australia. Dec. 1995.
Kulatunga, I. G., and Athula Arnarasekera. "Abhayagiri Vihara." Virtual Library - Sri Lanka. Web. 12 Oct. 2009. <http://www.lankalibrary.com/heritage/abayagiri.htm>.
Law, Bimala Churn. On the Chronicles of Ceylon. Calcutta: Royal Asiatic Society of Bengal, 1947. Print.
Lochtefeld, James G. The Illustrated Encyclopedia of Hinduism. New York: Rosen, 2002. Print.
Malalasekera, G. P. Dictionary of Pali Proper Names. London: Published for the Pali Text Society by Luzac &, 1960. Print.
Malavige, G. N., Rostron, T., Seneviratne, S. L., Fernando, S., Sivayogan, S., Wijewickrama, A. and Ogg, G. S. (2007), HLA analysis of Sri Lankan Sinhalese predicts North Indian origin. International Journal of Immunogenetics, 34: 313–315. doi: 10.1111/j.1744-313X.2007.00698.x
Menon, A. Sreedhara. A Survey of Kerala History. Kottayam: Sahitya Pravarthaka Co-operative Society ; National Book Stall, 1967. Print.
Middleton, John. World Monarchies and Dynasties. Armonk, NY: Sharpe Reference, 2005. Print.
Mullins, Mark R. "Dharma World Buddhist Magazine." Dharma World Buddhist Magazine. Dharma World, July 2007. Web. 24 July 2016.
Nilakanta Sastri K., & R. Champakalakshmi. A History of South India: From Prehistoric times to the Fall of Vijayanagar. New Delhi: Oxford UP, 1975. Print.
Obeyesekere, Donald. Outlines of Ceylon history. New Delhi: Asian Educational Services, 1999. Print. First Published in 1911
Obeyesekere, Gananath. "Buddhism, Ethnicity and Identity: A Problem of Buddist History." Journal o Buddist Ethics 10 (2003). Web. 10 Oct. 2009.
Oldenberg, Hermann. The Dîpavamsa. London: n.p., 1879. Print.
Paranavitana, Senarat, Leelananda Prematilleka, Kārttikēcu Intirapālā, and Lohuizen-De Leeuw J. E. Van. Senarat Paranavitana Commemoration Volume. Leiden: Brill, 1978. Print.
Paranavitana, Senarat. Art of the Ancient Singhalese. Colombo: Lake House Investments Ltd, 1971. Print.

Paranavitana, Senarat. Glimpses of Ceylon's Past. Colombo: Lake House, 1972. 34-41. Print.
Paranavitana, Senarat. Sinhalayo. Colombo: Lake House Investments, 1967. Print.
Parker, Henry. Ancient Ceylon. New Delhi: Asian Educational Services, 1992. Print.
Peiris, W. Karu. Abhayagiri Vihara Complex (n.d.): n. pag. Web. 22 July 2014.
Perera, A. D. "Upalvan, the Patron God of the Sinhalese." Encyclopedia of Buddhism, Ceylon 1&2 4 (1971): 88-104. Print.
Perera, D. T. "Colossal Buddha images of ancient Sri Lanka." InfoLanka. Web. 17 Dec. 2009. <http://www.infolanka.com/org/srilanka/hist/13.htm>.
Perera, D. T. "Elara, King of Anuradhapura." Vidyodaya University Journal 3.2 (1970). Lanka Library Forum. 21 Dec. 2008.
Pieris, Kamalika. "Historical Information from Inscriptions." Daily News Online Edition - Sri Lanka. Daily News Sri Lanka, 17 Oct. 2009. Web. 28 Aug. 2016.
Pieris, Kamalika. "Urban planning and transport in ancient and medieval Sri Lanka." Lanka Library Forum. June 2007.
Pollock, Sheldon I. Literary Cultures in History: Reconstructions from South Asia. Berkeley: U of California, 2003. Print.
Ponnamperuma, Senani. The Story of Sigiriya. Melbourne: Seelanka Media, 2014. Print.
Ramaswamy, Vijaya. Historical Dictionary of the Tamils. Lanham, MD: Scarecrow, 2007. Print.
Ranaweera, Munidasa P. "Ancient Stupas in Sri Lanka – Largest Brick Structures in the World." Construction History Society Newsletter 70 (2004). Print.
Ranaweera, Munidasa, and Gamunu Silva. "Conservation and Restoration of Ancient Stupas in Sri Lanka" Tenth East Asia-Pacific Conference on Structural Engineering & Construction – EASE (2006)
Ranaweera, Munidasa, and Helarisi Abeyruwan. Materials used in the construction, conservation, and restoration of ancient stupas in Sri Lanka. Proc. of Second International Congress on Construction History, Queen's College, Cambridge, UK. Peradeniya: Department of Civil Engineering, University of Peradeniya, 2006. Print.
Ratnasinghe, Aryadasa. "Dipavamsa and Mahavamsa." Dipavamsa and Mahavamsa. The Island, 28 May 1998. Web. 21 Mar. 2014.
Ratnasinghe, Aryadasa. "Disparity between Dipavamsa and Mahavamsa." Sinhala Jukebox Community. Daily News, 11 May 2004.
Ray, H. C., and De Silva K. M. History of Ceylon. Colombo: Ceylon UP, 1959. Print.
Reginald Farrar, Reginald. In Old Ceylon. London: Edward Arnold, 1908. Print.
Ring, Trudy, Robert M. Salkin, Paul Schellinger, & Sharon E. La Boda. International Dictionary of Historic Places: Asia and Oceania. Chicago: Dearborn, 1996. Print.
Ross, Russell R., and Andrea M. Savada. Sri Lanka: A Country Study. Washington: Federal Research Division, Library of Congress, 1988. Print.
Saha, N. "Blood Genetic Markers in Sri Lankan Populations—reappraisal of the Legend of Prince Vijaya." American Journal of Physical Anthropology 76.2 (1988): 217-25. Print.
Sen, Sailendra Nath. Ancient Indian History and Civilization. New Delhi: Wiley Eastern, 1988. Print.
Senaveratna, John M. Royalty in Ancient Ceylon: During the Period of the "great Dynasty" New Delhi: Asian Educational Services, 2005. Print.
Senaveratna, John M. The Date of Buddha's Death and Ceylon Chronology. Vol. XXIII. Colombo: J.R.A.S (Ceylon), 1913. Print.
Senaveratna, John M. The Story of the Sinhalese: From the Most Ancient times up to the End of "The Mahavasna", or Great Dynasty ; Vijaya to Maha Sena (B.C. 543 to A.D. 302). Colombo: W.M.A. Wahid, 1930. Print.
Siddhartha, R. "Mahanama in the Pali Literature." The Indian Historical Quarterly 8:3 1932.09 pp 462-465.
Silva, K. M. De. A History of Sri Lanka. New York: Penguin Books, 2005. Print.
Singh, Upinder. A History of Ancient and Early Medieval India: From the Stone Age to the 12th Century. New Delhi: Pearson Education, 2008. Print.
Smith, Bardwell L., and Holly Baker. Reynolds. The City as a Sacred Center: Essays on Six Asian Contexts. Leiden: E.J. Brill, 1987. Print.
Smither, James G. Architectural remains, Anurādhapura, Sri Lanka comprising the dāgabas and certain other ancient ruined structures. Polgasovita, Sri Lanka: Academy of Sri Lankan Culture, 1993. Print.
South Indian Inscriptions Volume_3 - Tiruvalangadu Copper-plates of Rajendra-Chola Inscriptions @ Whatisindia.com. South Indian Inscriptions Volume_3 - Tiruvalangadu Copper-plates of Rajendra-Chola Inscriptions @ Whatisindia.com. The Indian Analyst, 2007. Web. 22 July 2016.
Spencer, Jonathan. Sri Lanka: History and the Roots of Conflict. London: Routledge, 1990. Print.
Spittel, R. L. Far-Off Things. Colombo: Sooriya, 2001. Print.
Tennent, James E. Ceylon: an account of the island physical, and topographical. Vol. 1. London: Longman, Green, Longman and Roberts, 1859. Print.
The Cultural Triangle of Sri Lanka. [Paris]: UNESCO Pub., 2004. Print.
The Editors of Encyclopædia Britannica. "Rājāvaliya (historical Ceylonese Chronicle)." Encyclopedia Britannica Online. Encyclopedia Britannica, n.d. Web. 10 July 2014.
Turnour, George. The Mahawanso (Mahavasa) in Roman Characters, with the Translation Subjoined. Ceylon: Cotta Church Mission, 1837. Print.
Upham, Edward, ed. He Mahavansi, the Raja-ratnacari, and the Raja-vali : forming the sacred and historical books of Ceylon. Vol. 2. London: Parbury, Allen, and Co, 1833. Print.
Violatti, Cristian. "The Dates of the Buddha." The Dates of the Buddha. Ancient History Encyclopedia, 2 May 2013. Web. 27 July 2016.
Weerasooriya, Hubert E. Historical Guide to Anuradhapura's Ruins. New Delhi: Asian Educational Services, 1995. Print.
Wickramasinghe, Chandima S. Coloured Slavery in Ceylon (Sri Lanka). Vol. 54. Colombo: He Journal of the Royal Asiatic Society, 2008. N. pag. Print.
Williams, Harry. Ceylon; Pearl of the East. London: Robert Hall Limited, 1963. 75-99. Print.
Wright, Arnold, ed. Twentieth Century Impressions of Ceylon. New Delhi: Asian Educational Services, 2004. Print.
Zvelebil, Kamil. Companion Studies to the History of Tamil Literature. Leiden: Brill, 1992. Print.

Photographs

The photographs and illustrations used in this book are by the author with the exception of those cited below.

The Arival of Vijay - Ariyawansa Weerakkody; Maps of India and Sri Lanka - mapsofindia.com; Isurimuniya Jopseph Lawton photograph 1870 - Victoria and Albert Museum, London; Moon-stone (Sandakada pahana), Anuradhapura, Sri Lanka - Bernand Gagnon; Ruins of Abayagiri Vihara - British Library; Sigiriya Fresco Girl with Flowers, Mihintale Steps,Seated Buddha,Mihintale Steps - Sandie Mumme ; Ceramic storage jars ; Sri Lankan Customs;Seated Buddah corroded - https://www.lempertz.com/en/catalogues/lot/1072-1/294-a-gilt-bronze-figure-of-a-buddha-sri-lanka-anuradhapura-6th/7th-century.html; Wall painting at- Kelaniya Temple of Princess Hemamali and her husband Anuradha Dullewe Wijeyeratne, Public Domain, https://en.wikipedia.org/w/index.php?curid=34132905; Metropolitan Museum of Art, New York www.metmuseum.org - Seated Buddha Expounding the Dharma, Standing Bodhisattva probably Avalokiteshvara; Tara Bodhisattvi Foto, CC BY-SA 3.0, https://de.wikipedia.org/w/index.php?curid=5547764 - Von Pilifip Eigenes; Birmingham Museum of Art Bodhisattva Avalokitesvara [CC BY 3.0 (http://creativecommons.org/licenses/by/3.0)], via Wikimedia Commons -Sean Pathasema ; Elephant Plowing http://www.meryratio.hu/utazas-kelet-indiakon ;Ivory Carving of a King and Entourage Mounted on a War Elephant – Bayerische Schlösserverwältung www.residenz-muenchen.de; Dancing Ardhanarisvara – Sirima Kiribamune; Stupa Reliquary, Sri Lanka, The James W. and Marilynn Alsdorf Collection. © Michael Tropea; Rock crystal reliquary, 307-267 BC, Victoria & Albert Museum; Terracotta figurine, Sri Lanka, Victoria & Albert Museum; Head, perhaps of a Deity. 5th–6th century. Terracotta, The Metropolitan Museum of Art; Head, perhaps of a Deity. 7th–8th century. Granite, The British Museum; A female deity (Tārā), The British Museum; Prajnaparamita, Victoria & Albert Museum;Snake Lamp, Sri Lankan Customs

www.ingramcontent.com/pod-product-compliance
Lightning Source LLC
Chambersburg PA
CBHW040732020526
44112CB00059B/2948